THE
ASSISTANT
PRINCIPAL 50

Other Books by Baruti K. Kafele

The Aspiring Principal 50: Critical Questions for New and Future School Leaders

Is My School a Better School BECAUSE I Lead It?

The Principal 50: Critical Leadership Questions for Inspiring Schoolwide Excellence

The Teacher 50: Critical Questions for Inspiring Classroom Excellence

Closing the Attitude Gap: How to Fire Up Your Students to Strive for Success

Motivating Black Males to Achieve in School & in Life

THE
ASSISTANT
PRINCIPAL 50

Critical Questions *for* Meaningful Leadership and Professional Growth

BARUTI K. KAFELE

ASCD
Alexandria, Virginia USA

1703 N. Beauregard St. • Alexandria, VA 22311-1714 USA
Phone: 000-933-2723 or 703-578-9600 • Fax: 703-575-5400
Website: www.ascd.org • E-mail: member@ascd.org
Author guidelines: www.ascd.org/write

Ranjit Sidhu, *CEO & Executive Director*; Stefani Roth, *Publisher*; Genny Ostertag, *Director, Content Acquisitions*; Julie Houtz, *Director, Book Editing & Production*; Joy Scott Ressler, *Editor*; Judi Connelly, *Senior Art Director*; Thomas Lytle, *Associate Art Director*; Keith Demmons, *Production Designer*; Kelly Marshall, *Manager, Production Services*; Shajuan Martin, *E-Publishing Specialist*; Isel Pizarro, *Production Specialist*.

All web links in this book are correct as of the publication date below but may have become inactive or otherwise modified since that time. If you notice a deactivated or changed link, please e-mail books@ascd .org with the words "Link Update" in the subject line. In your message, please specify the web link, the book title, and the page number on which the link appears.

PAPERBACK ISBN: 978-1-4166-2944-3   ASCD product #121018   n5/20

PDF E-BOOK ISBN: 978-1-4166-2946-7; see Books in Print for other formats.

Quantity discounts are available: e-mail programteam@ascd.org or call 800-933-2723, ext. 5773, or 703-575-5773. For desk copies, go to www.ascd.org/deskcopy.

Library of Congress Cataloging-in-Publication Data

Names: Kafele, Baruti K., author.
Title: The assistant principal 50: critical questions for meaningful
   leadership and professional growth / by Baruti K. Kafele.
Other titles: Assistant principal fifty
Description: Alexandria, Virginia: ASCD, 2020. | Includes bibliographical
   references and index.
Identifiers: LCCN 2020002570 (print) | LCCN 2020002571 (ebook) | ISBN
   9781416629443 (paperback) | ISBN 9781416629467 (pdf)
Subjects: LCSH: Assistant school principals--United States. | Educational
   leadership--United States. | School management and organization--United
   States.
Classification: LCC LB2831.92.K339 2020 (print) | LCC LB2831.92 (ebook)
   | DDC 371.2/012--dc23
LC record available at https://lccn.loc.gov/2020002570
LC ebook record available at https://lccn.loc.gov/2020002571

28 27 26 25 24 23 22 21 20   2 3 4 5 6 7 8 9 10 11 12

The Assistant Principal 50 *is dedicated to every assistant principal who will read this book. Your job, though not an easy one, can certainly be rewarding. As I typically state and write, it is my strong contention that the assistant principalship is the most misunderstood and underutilized position in education. It is my hope that this book will lend further clarity to assistant principal efficiency and consistency.*

THE ASSISTANT PRINCIPAL 50

Critical Questions *for* Meaningful Leadership and Professional Growth

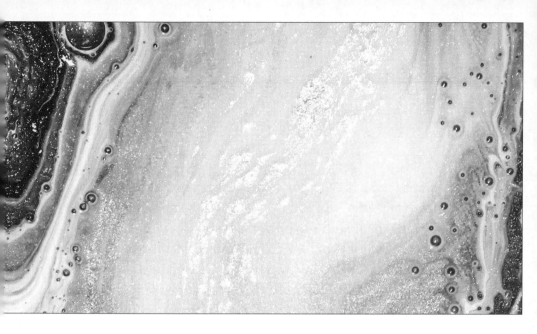

Acknowledgments

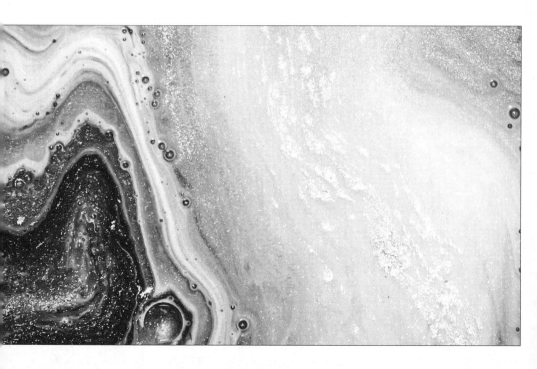

I want to thank Mrs. Joy Scott Ressler, my editor and the managing editor of this project, for bringing magic to both this book and my previous book, *The Aspiring Principal 50*; ASCD content acquisitions director Ms. Genny Ostertag, for believing in me for a long time now; and ASCD publisher Stefani Roth, for always having my back. I am immensely grateful for the three of you.

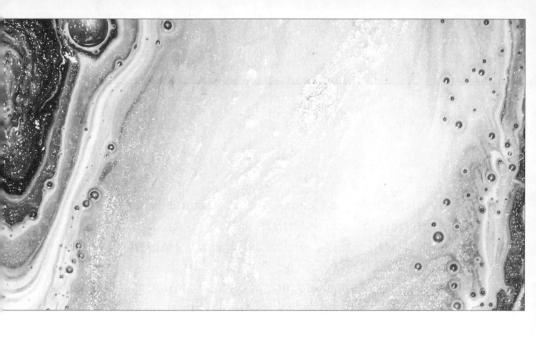

Introduction

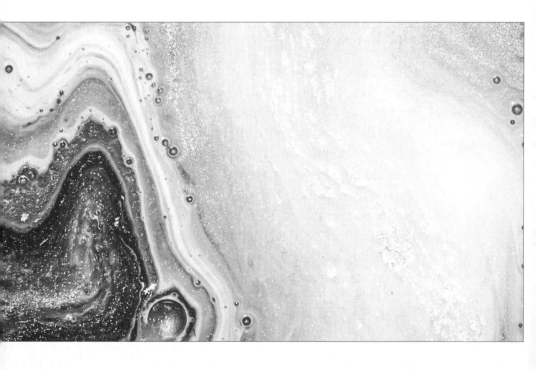

It's a beautiful early October Monday morning here in Montego Bay, Jamaica, as my wife Kimberly and I celebrate my 59th birthday. I'm sitting on my balcony and plan to read a few e-mails and check inboxes and DMs before I head to breakfast. As I read the messages, there are, as always, an abundance of queries about the assistant principalship from aspiring assistant principals (APs) and practicing APs. You see, two years ago, I created several YouTube videos aimed at preparing AP candidates for both the job interview and success once in the position. I didn't realize that creating those videos would position me as an authority on the assistant principalship (which was not my intent, although I welcome the role with open arms); I just wanted to do a good deed and make life easier for interviewees in light of the numerous questions I received about how to prepare for an AP interview or about situations that APs find themselves grappling with daily.

To further respond to the needs of aspiring principals and practicing APs, I wrote *The Aspiring Principal 50: Critical Questions for New and Future School Leaders* (ASCD) in early 2019. The purpose of that book was to help new and aspiring principals transition to the principalship. The book was also intended for assistant principals. Although I am extremely proud of that book, I knew that there was yet another perspective that I needed to address—the role of APs in their current capacities—because there is so much confusion about what an AP is and is not. In fact, a few months ago, I wrote a blog post entitled *The Assistant*

Principalship: The Most Misunderstood and Underutilized Position in Education. Of the more than 50 blog posts I have written over the years, that one was by far the most widely read. It resonated with countless APs throughout the United States and became the motivation for this book, *The Assistant Principal 50.*

Assistant principals must be utilized effectively and maximally. When the AP is, for example, reduced to serving as a disciplinarian, everyone—the principal, the staff members that the AP supervises and, most importantly, the students—loses (a matter that I'll discuss in detail in the book).

In keeping with my previous six ASCD books, at the core of *The Assistant Principal 50* are self-reflective questions. *The Assistant Principal 50* is a vehicle for you to study your "game film." In the world of sports, the study, analysis, breakdown, and dissection of the film from the game last played is crucial in preparing for the next opponent. It works the same way in education. Educators must study, analyze, break down, and dissect their "film." These questions will serve as your film. I want you to look at each question and ask yourself, "How does this question relate to my work as an assistant principal?", "How does this question relate to my growth and development as an assistant principal?", "How does this question relate to my effectiveness as an assistant principal?", "In what ways do I need to rethink what I am doing as an assistant principal?", "What adjustments do I need to make as an assistant principal?", "What do I currently do effectively as an assistant principal?", and "How will this question one day prepare me for the principalship?" It is my desire that these questions create discomfort, tension, and uneasiness for those who need to adjust their overall AP leadership. Discomfort, tension, and uneasiness are great motivators for change. When one feels comfortable in their lack of productivity, everyone loses. But if one can spark discomfort for another individual within their comfort of low productivity, there is a much higher probability for immediate change. I, therefore, want this book to serve as a vehicle toward creating discomfort for readers.

I am writing *The Assistant Principal 50* in the second person. I am speaking directly to you. I am having a one-on-one "conversation" with you. To make the book authentic and relevant and to "bring it to life," it is replete with my personal experiences as an AP and as a principal working with APs. All of my books are short and readable because, as a former AP and principal, I know exactly how hard you work and the incredibly long hours that you put into your craft daily. Although I kept it simple to read, I implore you to treat it as a book to read *and* to reference throughout your assistant principalship. And when you one day become a principal, I encourage you to use it as one of the tools in your toolbox to train your APs.

I anticipate that many principals will read this book. There are some hard truths in this book for principals. When APs aren't being developed properly, you don't have to look too far to understand why. It's typically what the principal is doing or is not doing. The principal must treat the assistant principalship as an extension of the graduate school program relative to their AP's continued professional growth and development. The AP is in place to both assist the principal and to be trained to one day step into the role of principal as seamlessly as possible.

Lastly, as my goal for this book is to completely transform "the most misunderstood and underutilized position in education," I could not confine the readership to assistant principals and principals. It is my hope and intent that this book be utilized widely by aspiring assistant principals; school districts; professors and graduate school administrators in education leadership departments within and outside of the United States who prepare students for school leadership (as while educational leadership programs typically prepare students to become effective *principals*, in most cases, one becomes an assistant principal before becoming a principal); and district-level superintendents and assistant superintendents.

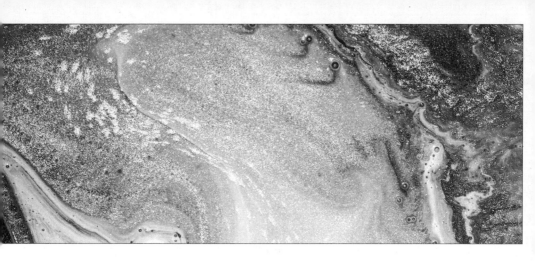

CHAPTER

The Assistant Principalship: What Is It?

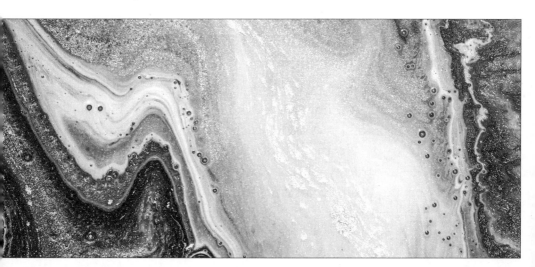

The title of this chapter is *The Assistant Principalship: What Is It?* I have pondered this question for the past 21 years. I have a solid grasp of what the assistant principalship is, what it isn't, and what it should never be. Because my work as a consultant takes me into hundreds of schools, I get to witness the various ways that APs are utilized, underutilized, and misutilized. This leaves me to conclude that there simply isn't a clear definition nationwide (or even statewide in any given state) of the title Assistant Principal. It is my strong belief that, toward maximizing the role of the AP, there must be a clear and consistent definition of Assistant Principal.

That is not to say that all APs must be utilized in the same manner across the United States, because different schools and districts have different needs. But when I see APs relegated to being full-time school disciplinarians, it becomes patently clear to me that there is confusion about the role of the AP, which takes me to our first question.

Q1 How do I define the assistant principalship?

When I ask you how you define the assistant principalship, I'm asking, "What does the assistant principalship mean to *you*?" In the Fall of 1994, I enrolled in graduate school to earn my M.A. in Education Administration to secure the position of Principal, *not* Assistant Principal.

The graduate school courses that I took over the course of two years trained and prepared me to think as a *principal*. Although I was clear on the sequence of becoming an assistant principal first, quite frankly, the assistant principalship was not on my radar because it wasn't discussed in my graduate school courses. The focus of the graduate school program was the principalship. The assistant principalship didn't fully make it onto my radar until I began to apply for positions. Even in the interviews, I vividly recall thinking as a principal, although I had the correct responses for the assistant principalship. Ultimately, I landed the position of Assistant Principal at a middle school and mid-year transitioned from my 5th grade classroom to the assistant principalship. My first day as an AP was January 2, 1998.

I went into the AP position completely "blind." Having since 1988 served as an elementary teacher, my only frame of reference of an AP was the four APs under whom I served in the two schools in which I taught. They were so different from one another and none of them practiced true *instructional leadership*. From my standpoint, what they had in common was that they were disciplinarians. Therefore, my definition of the assistant principalship was rooted in the leadership demonstrated by those four individuals. As a result, I entered the assistant principalship without a solid model of *effective* AP leadership.

How do you define assistant principal leadership? What does effective assistant principal leadership look like to you? When you think of the title Assistant Principal, what thoughts does it generate? A good starting place toward effective AP leadership is a clear and consistent definition of Assistant Principal based on what the position means to you.

Q2 Is my assistant principalship all that I conceptualized it would be?

Let me answer this question for myself first: *No!* In fact, I would answer with an *emphatic* no! I have articulated and written extensively over the years that the worst experience that I had in education was my very short tenure as an AP. Although I had no clear and consistent definition of the title Assistant Principal, I developed during my tenure as an AP a definition of what an AP was not.

During my tenure as an AP, my primary responsibility was student discipline. I was a full-time disciplinarian. That consumed my entire day, rooted in the climate and culture of the school. (I typically liken discipline to a micro issue and climate/culture to a macro issue.) In my school, we were so focused on the micro via me as school disciplinarian that we completely "missed the bus" on the macro—the climate and culture of the school. Consequently, from the time students entered the building until dismissal, my days were spent reading disciplinary referrals, lecturing and counseling students who were sent to me, and making decisions relative to the consequences of the actions outlined in the disciplinary referrals. During lunch period, I served as the supervisor of the cafeteria. After lunch period, I resumed my role as disciplinarian.

I also served as the teacher supply inventory clerk. (As I write this early in the morning on my balcony in Montego Bay, Jamaica, I have a wide smile on my face. However, the smile is one of disgust—a "smh," if you will. I'm reminiscing about the system that was put in place in my school where, in my capacity as AP, I maintained the supplies and photocopy paper inventory in a storage room. Teachers sent me requisitions daily and, when I wasn't disciplining students, I pushed a cart around the school delivering supplies and copy paper to teachers' classrooms—the second of my three core responsibilities as a AP.)

My third core responsibility was bus duty. Because our district was a magnet school district, our students came in from all over the city. My job was to greet the students in the morning (a good thing), get them settled, and see them off in the afternoon (also a good thing). (I will elaborate further on each of these in Chapter 7.)

The foregoing encapsulates how my days as an AP were spent, which was a far cry from what I'd envisioned based on what I'd learned in graduate school. Although I had no clear and consistent definition of what an Assistant Principal was, I never could have imagined that it was going to be like what I'd experienced. As I have looked back on the experience over the past two decades, it continues to pain me that because of the way that my role as AP was defined, the 30 teachers that I was to have supervised received little to no supervision from me. That translated to disaster for the students because both effective and ineffective teachers were being rewarded because as the teachers' evaluator of record, I was not in position to assist teachers with professional growth and development.

Is your assistant principalship all that you conceptualized it would be? Does your school culture enable you to do the things as a leader that your graduate school courses prepared you for? Are you being utilized optimally? Is your presence an asset to the teachers you supervise? Is your presence an asset to the students you lead? Are you being exposed to all facets of school leadership? The answers to these questions are vitally important because your position —Assistant Principal—is a vital one toward the overall success of *any* school.

Q3 Do I understand that the core of the assistant principalship is to assist the principal, *not* lead the school?

As I reflect on the inquiries I've received from APs over the years about the role of the AP, many of them are rooted in this question. A question I receive may be, for example, "Principal Kafele, I have so many ideas about how the school can be better for the children, but the principal is set in ways that are, in my mind, outdated. What can I do?" My answer to such a question is

> As one of the administrative leaders of your school, you have the ear of your principal. It is crucial that you earn the trust of your principal. In other words, in addition to your work ethic,

following directions effectively, demonstrating loyalty, and taking the initiative in those areas that fall within your "lane," you must have strong people skills. I repeat: *You must have strong people skills!* To convince your principal that your ideas will benefit your school, your people skills must be solid enough for you to be able to develop a cohesive bond/productive working relationship with your principal—which is absolutely crucial. How you communicate with your principal matters. You must make developing a strong relationship with your principal one of your top priorities within your overall leadership. You'll want to strive to develop an unbreakable trust between yourself and your principal so that you put the principal in a position to believe in you and the ideas that you bring to the table.

Regarding the question at hand—*Do I understand that at the core of the assistant principalship is to assist the principal, not lead the school*—I hear numerous concerns, complaints, and criticisms from APs about their principals. What the APs are essentially saying is that they can't get done the things that they'd like to get done because of what they describe as the ineffectiveness of their principal. This is a very delicate and sensitive situation to be in, particularly when there is a semblance of truth to it. As a starting point, my reminder to APs is

You are *not* the principal of the school! Again: You are *not* the principal! You are the Assistant

Principal and the line between you and the principal can never get blurred. You are there to *assist* the principal, not *lead* the school. Your time to lead your own school as principal (should you wish to do so) will come. In the meantime, as the Assistant Principal, your job is to learn, grow, develop as a school leader, and assist the principal in all ways possible.

All principal–assistant principal relationships are different. In an ideal principal–assistant principal relationship, as an AP, you are given the latitude and flexibility to grow and all of your ideas and suggestions for change and improvement are welcomed. However, not all principal–assistant principal relationships are ideal. Some can be quite complex, difficult, or even toxic. (We will dig much deeper into the principal–assistant principal dynamic in Chapter 3.) For now, the point of this question is to remind you to always keep at the forefront of your mind that, despite the challenges you may face in a less-than-favorable relationship with your principal, you are *not* the leader of the school. Your job is to assist the principal. You are the *Assistant Principal*.

Q4 Am I a career assistant principal or am I an aspiring principal?

This is an important question for any AP because it has direct implications for one's outlook on the current role. One who is content with being a career AP (or at least not desirous of the principalship) will more than likely approach the assistant principalship very differently from one who views the assistant principalship as a stepping-stone to the principalship.

As an AP, despite my very limited exposure to the larger picture of school leadership, I was "hungry." Nothing about me was career-AP oriented. I was hungry and wanted the principalship . . . badly. I wanted the role of Principal like nobody's business! Although I was relegated to being a full-time disciplinarian, I didn't allow myself to be or feel defeated. I went above and beyond in everything I did and learned everything I could about principal leadership. I was not exposed to the school budget, so I sought information about school budgeting outside of my school. I was not exposed to master scheduling, so I taught myself how to develop a master schedule. I went the extra mile and learned on my own any aspect of school leadership to which I hadn't been exposed. Why? Because I was "hungry!" I wanted to be a building principal. I wanted nothing more professionally than to lead a school of my own.

Looking back, had I been content being an AP and spent my tenure assisting the principal, I imagine that I would have approached my assistant principalship quite differently and viewed it through a different set of lenses than I did. I may even have been content being a school disciplinarian. But because of my leadership aspirations, I wanted everything that school leadership had to offer.

Who are you as an assistant principal? How long have you been an assistant principal? What are your aspirations as a school leader? Do you aspire to become a principal? Are you "hungry" to become a principal? Do you want the principalship, like, yesterday? Are you content in your current role as Assistant Principal? Is the assistant principalship satisfying and fulfilling for you?

If you're hungry to become a principal, you must think as a principal . . . *now*. You must see yourself in that position . . . *now*. You must interpret all the stimuli around you within the building as though you are the principal. You must do these things without trying to function as the principal. Look at all situations as if you were the principal and consider how you would respond/react to everything imaginable if, in fact, you were the principal of your school.

If you are a career AP or simply content in your current role, my advice to you is to simply do your job to the best of your ability. Be the best version of yourself every time you walk into your school. Not everyone desires to become a principal. Everyone isn't built to be a principal. Everyone doesn't have the temperament to be a principal. Everyone doesn't have the time to be a principal given the high number of hours, during the week and on weekends, that principals must devote to their work to be effective. Everyone has a life outside of school and, for some, the balance between life outside of school and life as a principal could be challenging if not impossible. The bottom line is this: you must determine whether you're an aspiring principal or a career assistant principal/content in your role (because of the implications for your work, preparation, goals, aspirations, and your overall peace of mind).

Q5 Do I regularly engage in my own professional learning toward being an effective assistant principal?

Closely associated with the previous question, I'm now asking you about your ongoing preparation toward being an effective AP, regardless of whether you are an aspiring principal or a career AP. How much of yourself do you pour into your preparation toward effective assistant principal leadership? How much time do you devote to reading and studying school leadership? How effective are you as an assistant principal? How beneficial are you to the staff you supervise? How beneficial are you to the students that you lead? How beneficial are you to your principal? Also, how beneficial are you to the parents of your students? These questions are critical for anyone in school leadership. I want you to consider how beneficial you are to your entire school community.

The qualities that you bring to the assistant principalship as a human being—the characteristics that make up who you are—are vital. Toward developing solid relationships and being an asset to all of the stakeholders in your school, you must be one of great character who genuinely cares and wants students and staff to soar to the best of their abilities. The aspect of your character that I want to focus on here is your preparation for leadership success and your work ethic—not how hard you work, but how smart you work. The *quality* of your work. We've both observed many who work extremely hard but make very little progress—those who put in long hours and perhaps work seven days a week. However, putting in countless hours does not always result in progress. Hard work must be coupled with working smart.

Earlier in this chapter, I stated that all principals are different and that the differences will have implications for you regarding what you are exposed to as an AP. Having superior people skills can be beneficial as regards what you are exposed to as an AP. But let's say that you are in a very difficult, challenging, undesirable, and tension-filled relationship with your principal and that you have determined, unequivocally, that it is not of your making and that there's nothing you can do about it. If that is the case, for the sake of staff, students, and parents, you must, nevertheless, continually grow and be effective as an AP. Your staff and students are relying on you, so you can't afford to throw up your hands in disgust. You must continue to strive to be amazing in your capacity as an AP, despite any obstacles you may encounter. You must be an open book with eyes and ears wide open as you strive to take in and learn all that you can. You must approach your position as one who desires to be a guru in school leadership in general and AP leadership in particular. You must purposefully observe everything you can about your principal's leadership. You must study your principal and determine which of her actions are useful to you and which are of no use to you. You must treat your principal as if she were an ongoing graduate school course on school leadership. You must read everything you can get your hands on and watch videos about leadership in general and school leadership in particular. You must participate in a variety of professional learning networks (PLNs), actively participate on a social media platform, and be a part of a network of fellow APs (which I will discuss further in the following section). You must be an AP leadership sponge who absorbs as much information as you possibly can. This translates to your professional learning being a high priority toward your overall growth and development to becoming an extraordinary AP.

Q6 How often do I get to collaborate, "compare notes," and exchange ideas with other assistant principals?

Now this is a question that I probably couldn't speak about enough. Assistant principal networks are *vital*. I often say that the principalship has got to be one of the loneliest and thankless positions on the planet. Our "thank-yous" come through the successes our schools experience under our leadership. Well, I feel the same way about the assistant principalship—times 10! In far too many cases, though not all, APs are relegated to doing the "dirty work"—doling out discipline, cafeteria duty, bus duty, and so on. This is not necessarily work that generates a line of people approaching you to say, "Thank you." Instead, the AP is often a person to be feared, and you didn't become a school leader to be feared. You became a school leader because you felt you had something to offer students and staff toward taking a school to heights previously unimagined.

Being consumed by the duties mentioned without a balance of the other important aspects of school leadership can be quite stressful. (Trust me, I know something about that. I dealt with so many disciplinary issues [as I was the sole disciplinarian in an urban middle school of 650 students] that I left the school stressed almost every day.) I knew that in my role as AP, I was to supervise half of the entire school staff, which included approximately 30 teachers. However, my discipline workload was so intense that I neglected my supervisory duties. I was not the instructional leader that I aspired to be. Instead, I was in the thankless role of school disciplinarian, and my staff and students suffered as a result.

In hindsight, I wish that I had taken the initiative and launched a network of APs within my district and in neighboring districts. The good thing is that these networks now exist in various districts across the United States. They give APs opportunities to collaborate with one another, compare notes, and exchange ideas. This is vital because unless you are interacting with others who do the same work that you do, you can easily be left with the impression that you are all alone and that no one else is toiling over these thankless duties the way that you are. Assistant principal networks can also be very revealing. There may be individuals in a network who have figured out how to simultaneously, for example, function as school disciplinarian and maximize their instructional leadership. These networks provide APs with endless opportunities to learn from one another. Sometimes, though, as human beings, we simply need like-minded people to whom to vent. (Family and friends who work in other capacities may not fully understand your frustrations, particularly if your salary is higher than theirs. They might tell you to "get over it.") Your fellow APs, however, fully understand your frustrations and sometimes just having an ear to hear them can soothe some of the pain. Do you network with other assistant principals? How often do you communicate and collaborate with assistant principal colleagues?

Remember, in the 21st century, networking need not always involve physically coming together. Social media platforms such as Twitter, and even text groups, enable folks to chat from wherever they are. If you are not a part of an AP's virtual network, you may want to start one with other APs or join existing groups via one of the various social media platforms.

Q7 Why do I lead?

Let's close this chapter by discussing your attitude as an AP. For those of you who are familiar with my work as a writer or presenter, you know that I have written and spoken extensively about the "attitude of the leader." When I write and speak about leadership practices, I typically start with the "attitude of the leader" because one's attitude in the pursuit of any endeavor is the essential starting place. An attitude of negativity, pessimism, doubt, or despair will not yield optimal results. Attitude is key. Attitude is vital toward attaining and sustaining maximum results.

A vital component toward sustaining a positive attitude during your assistant principalship is establishing a clearly defined purpose for leading. I am referring to your *why* and I am asking you, "What is your *why*?", "Have you established a *why*?", "Are you grounded in your *why*?", and "In your capacity as assistant principal, are you walking in your *why*?" As I have been saying for a couple of decades, the assistant principalship is a very confusing position, as evidenced by the wide variety of ways that assistant principals are utilized nationally. Because, as I state, the assistant principalship is the most misunderstood and underutilized position in education, it is the one position wherein one's purpose can become murky when transitioning from teacher to AP to principal.

As a classroom teacher, my *why*—which was rooted in the empowerment of African American and Latino boys— was clear. When I became a principal, I maintained my *why* throughout my years as the leader of four schools. It was during my assistant principalship that I lost my *why*. I completely lost my purpose because of a *perceived* inability to walk in it (noting my use of the word "perceived"). I am saying here that, in hindsight, I could have done things in such a way that would have enabled me to simultaneously effectively assist the principal and walk in my *why*. I here strongly suggest that if you are in a situation comparable to the one in which I found myself—that is, you were walking in your *why* as a classroom teacher (the leader of your classroom) but lost your autonomy as AP—that you never, ever allow yourself to lose sight of your *why*. It is the foundation of your assistant principalship and likely the reason you sought an administrative position. Although you might be using your assistant principalship as a stepping-stone to the principalship, as an AP, you must know that your students and the staff you supervise need you to be a strong AP and that will, in part, require that you walk in your *why*. Toward that end, you may have to examine how you are currently utilizing and managing your time; you and the other administrative leaders may need to take an honest look at the overall climate and culture of your school and determine whether it can be transformed; or you may need to examine other variables that may be preventing you from sustaining your *why*.

Each morning as you prepare mentally and emotionally for leadership, be sure to ask yourself, "Why do I lead?"and "Will I walk in my *why* today?" At the end of the day, ask yourself, "Why do I lead?" and "Did I walk in my *why* today?" If you don't answer the second question affirmatively at either point in the day, you've got to look deeply within yourself to determine why you didn't and what adjustments you will need to make so that the following day will be better. Your *why*, even as an AP, matters exponentially!

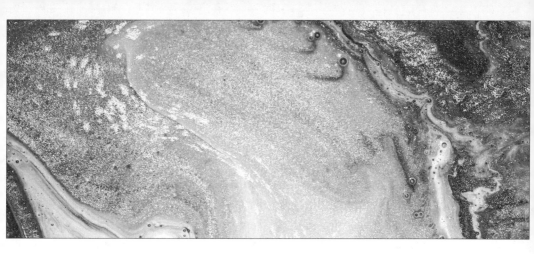

CHAPTER

2

"I'm an Instructional Leader, Too!"

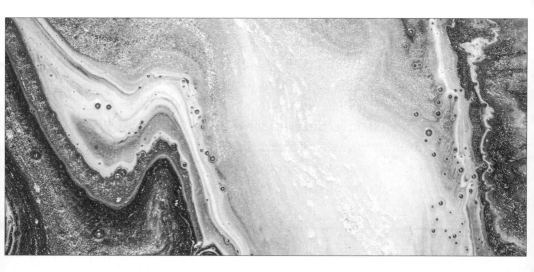

Before I was completely satisfied with the "finished product" that is this book, I spent several months creating, organizing, revising, and editing the eight chapter titles and 50 questions contained in this book. The chapter that most consumed my thoughts, energy, and emotions and is dearest to my heart—because it is all about instructional leadership, the heart and soul of school leadership—was this one.

Student learning and student achievement are the primary reasons that the school doors open every day. Everything we do are vehicles to get us to those two student-centered objectives. The question then is, how do we ensure that student learning and student achievement are occurring in our schools? As an administrative leader in your school and, in your case, as AP, the instructional aspect of your leadership is absolutely crucial. I repeat: *The instructional aspect of your leadership is absolutely crucial!* To that end, as I wrote the five questions contained in this chapter, I knew that I could discuss the ideas of each question under one overarching question because they are all so interconnected. But I decided that as the primary audience for this book is APs (and, thereby, likely a plethora of new school administrators), and as one who is fully committed to professional learning for school leaders, I should treat each idea embodied within these five self-reflective questions separately. Because your effectiveness as an instructional leader can be the difference between the success or failure of a child, I wanted to ensure that I was as thorough as possible in this chapter.

Q8 Is instructional leadership an inherent part of my day?

The question at hand is, Is instructional leadership an inherent part of my day? I want you to now deeply reflect on a typical day of leadership in your capacity as AP. Let the DVD of your mind spin and watch your day unfold as one of the leaders in your school in the context of this question. As you engage in this self-reflection of your typical day, I want you to hear me as you ponder the question. Now, I want you to assess your leadership, again within the context of the question. In other words, I want you to evaluate your performance relative to the role that instructional leadership plays on a typical day as an AP. As you engage in self-reflection and self-assessment, can you truly say that you are an instructional leader in your school? Can you truly say that instructional leadership is inherent in your overall assistant principal leadership? What is the evidence that you are an instructional leader?

As an AP, the success of both the staff you supervise and the students you lead demands that you be an effective instructional leader. There's simply no way around it. If you supervise at least one teacher, that teacher's students depend on your instructional leadership because, at the proverbial "end of the day," their success in the classroom depends on the effectiveness of their teacher. Hence, the question—is instructional leadership an inherent part of your day?

Q9 How do the teachers I supervise perceive me as an instructional leader?

Anyone can claim to be anything, but the facts will bear out the truth. In my mind, I was, both as an AP and in the first few years of my principalship, an instructional leader. In fact, in those first couple of years of my principalship, I thought that I was *the* instructional leader. Although I never asked the teachers I supervised whether they perceived me as an instructional leader, there is no doubt in my mind that any of them would have concluded that I was (although I was so deeply engrossed in discipline and engaging students that instruction had not made it onto my radar as my primary responsibility). As an AP, I spent the bulk of my time responding to disciplinary referrals and, as a new principal, I spent a lot of my time engaging with students in my attempt to motivate them and keep them motivated. Toward being perceived by teachers as an effective and beneficial instructional leader, I had a great deal of learning and growing to do.

How do the teachers you supervise perceive you as an instructional leader? Their perceptions of your leadership are their reality as it relates to your leadership. Said differently, their perceptions about your leadership matter toward your overall effectiveness as an instructional leader. Their perceptions are rooted in your actions toward their classroom instructional practices. Who are you relative to the instructional growth and development of the teachers you supervise? Why would they have reason to believe that you are an asset to their instructional practices and their ongoing growth and development? Do your teachers perceive you as a source of sound instructional strategies?

Whenever I conduct school leadership seminars, the following self-reflective question is central to all that address instructional leadership:

> Do I ensure that my staff utilize a variety of instructional strategies that take into account the different learning styles, ability levels, and social-emotional needs of my students in student-centered, culturally responsive, culturally relevant, and equitable learning environments?

Admittedly, this is a huge question and an entire day can be spent unpacking its various components. The question for you, though, is, how is this question applicable to your instructional leadership? Are you able to share appropriate instructional strategies with your teachers? Are you perceived by your teachers as a source of appropriate instructional strategies for their students? Are you well versed in good, sound instruction that benefits *all* learners?

How you are perceived by staff speaks volumes about the quality of the professional relationships you have developed with staff. Your goal must be to position yourself as instructional leader so that you will be *perceived* as an instructional leader. Said differently, your goal must be to position yourself as an instructional leader so that there is no mistake in your teachers' minds that they are better teachers *because* of the collegial relationship that they have with you. Let's now turn our attention to how to make this a reality in your leadership.

Q10 How important are pre- and post-observation conferences to my assistant principalship?

I continually reference APs who are primarily relegated to serving as disciplinarians. I have interacted with countless APs nationally over the past 15 years and, when talking about the responsibilities of an AP, the issue of discipline continually comes up. Many APs will tell me that the pre- and post-observation conferences are a virtual impossibility or unrealistic because of the amount of time they spend daily on other responsibilities (e.g., lunch duty in the middle of the day). Many APs who spend inordinate amounts of time serving as disciplinarians have confided to me that they are only able to spend time observing classroom instruction twice per year—when evaluations are due. While as a former AP I completely understand this reality, in the final analysis, it's a lose-lose situation for all parties— the students, the staff, *and* the assistant principal.

Looking back on my days as an AP, I recall feeling that I had zero time for pre- and post-observation conferences. In fact, I felt strongly that I had very little time to conduct classroom observations in general (because of the time that I spent handling student discipline issues). My reality forced me to rationalize that the pre-observation conferences were not that important and that when I had an opportunity to visit classrooms, I would simply make unannounced "cold calls." I wanted to get the "real deal" and felt that teachers would "put on a show" if they were prepared for my visit. Wow! I learned over time that my thinking and approach to classroom observations were flawed, outdated and, most of all, grossly counterproductive. It was a "gotcha" approach that in no way lent itself to helping teachers grow.

The whole idea of a classroom observation is formative—to help the teacher grow and develop through a truly collegial relationship with all teachers that you supervise. That translates to a methodical approach whereby the teacher and the administrator have an opportunity to discuss those areas of the teacher's practice on which both parties agree that the teacher can become stronger. Consequently, the pre-observation conference centers around the area or areas in which the administrator and teacher have mutually deemed that the teacher is deficient. The conversation focuses on strategies for improvement and both parties agree on a date and time that the administrator will visit the classroom to observe what was discussed. The administrator, while observing the teacher, isn't there to observe everything that the eye can see; this would be counterproductive. The administrator is there to observe solely what was discussed in the pre-observation conference. Finally, an appointment is made immediately following the observation (to enable the administrator to provide the teacher with feedback and schedule a follow-up visit).

As an AP, is the foregoing a part of your leadership reality? How important are pre- and post-observation conferences to your assistant principalship? As with most of the questions posed in this book, the culture of your school may have to be closely examined and shifted if your day does not allow you to sustain a collegial relationship with the teachers you supervise. If the culture of your school is preventing you from being the instructional leader that your teachers and students need, shifting the culture of your school must be high on your entire administrative team's list of priorities.

Q11 Is there a correlation between my supervision of teachers and their continual improvement in instruction?

As an AP, you more than likely supervise a variety of staff members who work in various capacities. Predicated on their capacities, their professional needs vary and you must possess the skill set to meet the professional needs of *all* staff. This will require a school culture that enables you to effectively simultaneously wear multiple hats throughout the day. Most of the staff you supervise, however, are teaching staff and, as they provide instruction to your students, they will invariably require the bulk of your attention.

The question as to whether there's a correlation between your supervision of teachers and their continual improvement in instruction is basically asking, is there a causal effect between your supervision of teachers and their performance in the classroom? Does your instructional leadership exist, and does it matter? I will now share (as I've widely shared in presentations and previous writings) what I was told by my mentor (who later became my direct supervisor when I became a principal) during my administrative internship in the mid-90s:

> Mr. Kafele, when you become an administrator, the purpose of your supervision of teachers will be their continual improvement in instruction.

Those words stayed with me . . . forever. They rang loudly in my ears throughout my assistant principalship and my principalship and inspired the writing of my book *Is My School a Better School BECAUSE I Lead It?* At day's end, as I reflected on the day, my primary thoughts centered around whether I visited classrooms (which included engaging in pre- and post-observation conferences) and the quality of classroom visits and conferences. If I hadn't engaged in any of those activities, I asked myself why. Every day as I engaged in self-reflection, my mentor's words drove my thinking because, as one who thought of himself as an instructional leader, I had to demonstrate to myself that I was indeed who and what I claimed to be. I had to demonstrate to myself that there was a correlation between my supervision and my teachers' continual improvement in instruction.

In your capacity as AP, is there a correlation between your supervision and your teaching staff's continual improvement in instruction? Are your teachers improving instructionally because of your direct supervision? Are your teachers growing in their practice because of your presence in the building? These are difficult questions that I challenge you to ask yourself daily. While your teachers can grow independent of your supervision—through solid professional development and a commitment to implementing what was learned or developing solid "thought partnerships" or collegial relationships with colleagues—there's nothing like a collegial relationship with a direct supervisor who is methodical and dedicated to helping teachers grow. As an AP, your focus must be on helping teachers grow; the teachers that you supervise cannot afford anything less. The success of your students depends on the continual growth and development of your teachers, which necessitates that you be the instructional leader that your teachers need you to be.

Q12 Am I a professional development resource for staff?

As an AP, in addition to being one of your school's instructional leaders, you are one of your school's "lead learners." You must *always* model professional learning for your staff. Your staff, particularly the staff you supervise, must see evidence that your professional learning *continued* and *intensified* after graduate school. *You can't perform your duties as an instructional leader optimally if you are not growing as a leader.* Education changes and evolves daily and, as an AP, you must grow and evolve along with it. Believe me when I say that if you don't grow, it shows (for example, in the way that you approach good practice in the classroom). As I type, it's the end of 2019. The classroom of 2009, just 10 short years ago, is virtually obsolete. The world has changed, society has changed, students have changed, and the strategies used to reach them have changed. Have you kept pace with the changes?

I am quite certain that there isn't a teacher you supervise who doesn't have room for pedagogical growth. As teachers' supervisor and evaluator of record, are you a professional development resource for your teachers? Do you provide your teachers with relevant resources toward their ongoing professional learning? Can your teachers look to you as a source of professional resources or information they may be seeking? As an instructional leader, you must position yourself to be able to recommend books, journals, websites, articles, blog posts, and the like for your teachers. Moreover, you should regularly provide your teachers with journal articles, education articles, and blog posts. It is imperative that you and your principal and the rest of the administrative team are in accord so that all staff receive the same information and that the information is discussed in staff meetings, professional learning communities, and so on.

You cannot afford to have your teachers see you in the stereotypical role of an AP—disciplinarian, cafeteria supervisor, and school bus supervisor. You must position yourself in such a way that your teachers see you as an educator—as one of them, as a source of professional learning, as an instructional leader. Your role is to keep your staff informed. Chances are that although staff may independently be engaged in reading educational literature toward enhancing their craft, they may not all be reading the same material. Although reading autonomously is not a bad thing, it is always good when some staff reading (and study) materials are common and that staff engage with one another toward better understanding the various concepts that they will, ultimately, implement collectively. Your role in facilitating this process is vital.

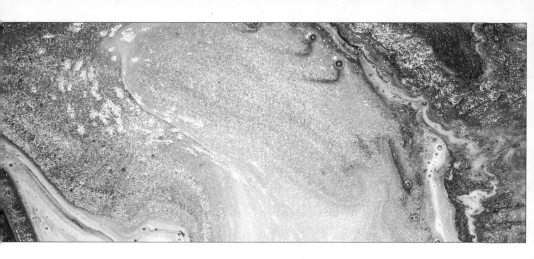

CHAPTER

3

The Principal–Assistant
Principal Relationship

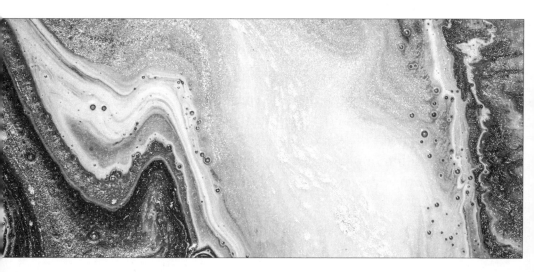

Q13 How often do I seek out my principal for advice, guidance, and direction toward becoming a better leader?

A few years ago, I recorded and posted on YouTube a couple of AP job interview videos; they rapidly amassed tens of thousands of views. In the videos, although I stated facetiously, "When you get hired, you better reach out to me to say thank-you," hundreds of newly hired APs did just that. After they thanked me, many followed with this question: What do I do now? Because so many newly hired APs wanted direction as to next steps, I recorded a follow-up video entitled, "You Got the Job ... NOW WHAT?" At the heart of my response was to go directly to the principal and engage in a dialogue relating to the principal's expectations for a newly hired AP. I wanted the APs to know that initially they are not expected to walk into their new assignment and start leading. Instead, they are to walk into that building and have a good, healthy, and productive conversation with the principal (which I anticipate will be initiated by the principal) as soon as possible.

What's key here is that the conversation can never end. The conversation, rather than occurring solely on the first day on the job or once in a while, must be ongoing. In addition to being in your school to assist, you are also there to learn—particularly if you are an aspiring principal.

Because your principal is one of your sources of information and professional learning, you must utilize him as a consistent source of leadership advice, guidance, and direction. Whether you are a new or seasoned AP, the advice, guidance, and direction that you receive from the principal never ends. As you become seasoned and effective in your work, although the frequency of the mentorship that you receive from the principal may decrease, in an ideal principal–assistant principal relationship, the principal will *always* be there to guide you in your capacity as both an AP and an aspiring principal. But what if you perceive the relationship with your principal to be less than ideal? What if you perceive your principal to be unapproachable? What if your relationship with your principal has become hostile or one in which communication and collaboration has all but disappeared? Because of the work that I do as a consultant, I often hear from APs and principals about principal–assistant principal relationships that have soured. And when the principal–assistant principal relationship sours or becomes toxic, the entire school loses. Let's talk more about this relationship in the next question.

Q14 How intentional am I about developing and maintaining a healthy, collegial relationship with my principal?

There's so much here that I think I can write an entire book on this question alone. I receive a plethora of e-mails from APs seeking advice on how to develop healthy and collegial relationships with their principals and from principals on how to develop healthy and collegial relationships with their APs. As one who served as both an AP and a principal, I can certainly identify with both leaders. Since this book is written for APs, I want to address relationship development and maintenance from their vantage point.

I cannot overstate or overemphasize the significance of your relationship with your principal. It can be the difference between the success or failure of your school. Leadership matters! Leadership is everything! Show me a school with the most effective teachers imaginable and less-than-effective leadership and I'll show you an underperforming school. Although a school with deficient leadership may not be failing, it certainly won't perform optimally. Now, show me a school with brand-new, fresh-out-of-college teachers with zero experience beyond student teaching and strong and effective leadership, and I'll show you a school with a wealth of potential to be phenomenal. Why? Because of the leadership and its understanding of the necessity of ongoing support, guidance, and direction for new staff.

But what if your relationship with your principal is less than favorable? What if you and your principal don't communicate? What if you and your principal don't collaborate? What if you and your principal don't trust each other? What if the principal is threatened by your presence? Such situations can translate to an environment of toxicity because when the leadership is at odds, it adversely impacts the entire building. Moreover, when the leadership isn't on the same page, it becomes blatantly obvious to staff—which can lead to a very complicated as well as toxic school environment.

As you read this and if by chance I'm speaking directly to your situation, you may be asking yourself, "But I'm only the assistant principal, not the principal, so what am I supposed to do?" My response is: Yes, you're not the principal, but your students and staff depend on the leadership functioning as a solid, cohesive, productive unit. This is where your people skills *must* kick in. Consider for a moment a high-performing car salesperson versus a low-performing car salesperson. If you ask a high-performing car salesperson their secret to success, I can assure you they are not going to tell you it's because they're experts in talking about the features and benefits of the cars they sell. Instead, they are going to tell you it's because of their commitment to developing relationships with their customers. It's the relationships that they develop in very short periods of time that enable them to sell cars at a high volume. Said differently, the application of their people skills enables them to be highly successful. Well, your people skills have implications for your relationship with your principal. Although you are not the principal, your people skills still matter. Your commitment to the relationship matters. Therefore, if you have a less-than-favorable relationship with your principal, don't get upset/shut down/throw in the towel. Instead, commit to developing a relationship with your principal.

Before moving on, I want to revisit a question I posed previously: What if the principal is threatened by your presence?

This is never healthy. While you *can't* control the feelings and perceptions of your principal, you *can* control yourself and your loyalty to your principal. As an AP and thereby an *assistant to the principal,* you must always strive to stay in your "assistant principal" lane and to never give the impression that you are trying to lead the school or undermine the principal. When you step out of your lane without the approval of your principal, you run the risk of jeopardizing your relationship with your principal. As an AP, your relationship with your principal must always be professional, productive, and honest. You must never engage in actions and behaviors that make your presence threatening to your principal, cause your principal to second-guess your loyalty, or compromise the relationship you have developed with your principal. Once the principal feels threatened or uncomfortable by your presence in your capacity as AP, the probability of you functioning as a team in the truest sense of the word will diminish exponentially.

Let's now explore how your relationship with your principal translates to you leading effectively.

Q15 Is my relationship with my principal conducive to my effectiveness as an assistant principal?

In Chapter 1, I discussed the difference between the principal and the AP. I stated that the principal is the leader of the school and that the job of the AP is to assist the principal. While a principal may provide an AP with opportunities to learn all facets of principal leadership, that does not translate to the AP assuming the role of principal of the school. The principal is still the principal and as an AP, you can't be confused about that. You will eventually have your opportunity to lead your own school (if you so wish), but you are not now the leader of the school. As an AP, you must assist and learn.

I often meet APs who feel they can lead their schools more effectively than their principals. That may very well be the case, but when the leadership lines get blurred, the result could be disastrous. When the AP attempts to be the leader of the school, the principal–assistant principal relationship inevitably breaks down or deteriorates—because the AP has stepped out of her lane. As an AP, you must always strive to simultaneously stay in your lane and seek to learn and do more. You want your relationship with your principal to be conducive to your overall effectiveness as an AP. You cannot be optimally effective if you are at odds or have a bitter relationship with the leader of the school. Always keep the goal of being an effective *assistant* principal at the forefront of your thinking while simultaneously utilizing your assist principalship as preparation or a "training ground" for your next position—AP at another school or principal.

Toward the overall effectiveness of APs, principals and APs must meet regularly. In this instance, I am not referring to meeting to seek advice, guidance, and direction toward becoming a better leader. Instead, I am referring to the requisite daily meetings that must occur between the principal and APs (and other teacher leaders in the building, when necessary) toward planning and strategizing each day and debriefing at the end of each day. While planning, strategizing, and debriefing can occur in the same meeting, the point here is that they must occur *regularly* (if not daily). I feel strongly that administrative leadership teams cannot be optimally effective if they don't regularly plan, strategize, and debrief about all aspects of the school. The meetings, whether prior to or at the end of the school day, must take place.

Q16 What is my relationship with the other administrative leaders on our leadership team?

In very small schools, principals are typically the only administrators in the building. Schools with between 500 to 1,000 students typically have at least one AP, and sometimes two. Large schools can have anywhere from two to six (or more) APs. As much as the principal more than likely appreciates the team of administrator assistants, the leadership and the management of the administrative team in and of itself can be challenging. Let's say, for example, that a large high school has four grade-level APs and two APs that serve in other than grade-level capacities (such as curriculum and assessment and special needs). For a principal, managing those administrators alone is comparable to running a small business of six employees—and that's not always an easy thing to do. Compound that with a school that comprises 200 employees and 3,000 students. All of that falls under the leadership of the principal. Leading a school (of 3,207, in this case) effectively is largely contingent on the effectiveness and the cohesion of the administrative team.

If you are one of two or more APs in your school, for the sake of the entire school, just as your relationship with your principal must be strong, your relationships with the other AP(s) must also be strong. That means that, as a team, ongoing communication is essential. Your administrative team must be unified. As you are not the principal, it is understood that you do not have authority over the team. What you do have authority over, however, is yourself. This means that you must always strive to do your part toward ensuring that the administrative team is unified. Are you an asset to the team and members of the team? Do you take the initiative to keep the lines of communication open with the other assistant principal(s)? Do you play your part in supporting and backing up your team members? Do you give advice to team members when appropriate? Are you open to receiving advice from your administrative colleagues? Do you regularly discuss the particulars of the school day, with an emphasis on classroom instruction, school climate, and school culture, while strategizing as to how best to meet the needs of your school? Do you and your team members study and learn together? As the sayings go, "Teamwork makes the dream work" and "There's no 'I' in team." That translates to the significance of your administrative team striving to operate as a strong, cohesive unit.

Q17 Do staff perceive that our leadership team is operating as a cohesive unit?

Question 16 addressed the relationships and cohesion between APs. This question will focus on the perceptions that staff may have of the entire administrative leadership team. It's one thing for the team to intentionally work toward functioning as a cohesive unit, but the message that unit conveys to the staff matters, too. The message conveyed must be, "We are one," even if there is conflict and disagreement between the members of the team. (Conflicts must remain in-house and be resolved as quickly as possible.) In any organization, department, or team, conflict and disagreement are inevitable. What's key is how and when they are resolved. When the leadership is in conflict, it has a way of adversely affecting an entire school.

Looked at differently, staff perceptions matter, too, and the leadership must always be cognizant of staff perceptions—because the perceptions that staff have of the leadership team become the reality of the leadership team. It is what others perceive, not what you say, that matters most. People act on their perceptions, not on what is said. When the leadership team is not in accord or divided, it is very easy for staff to manipulate—whether deliberately or unintentionally—the division. For example, toward disciplining a student, staff may be aware that the administration isn't on the same page regarding consequences administered and send a disciplinary referral to the AP who they perceive doles out harsh consequences. However, if all

APs are in accord, if consequences are warranted, there's a higher probability that an infraction will be handled uniformly regardless of to which AP a student is sent.

Staff perceptions aren't limited to behavioral infractions. Differences as to how APs address any and everything under their authority can be perceived as a lack of cohesion, consistency, and uniformity within the team. As one of a team of APs, it is imperative that you play your part toward ensuring that the team is functioning as a unified, cohesive unit. Issues that arise between you and an administrative colleague must remain in-house. Issues that become common knowledge to staff become problems within the team and may have schoolwide implications (because people outside of the administrative team are now privy to sensitive information). Again, it is fully understood that you are not the principal and your authority relative to the team is, therefore, limited. However, as you are in a very prominent and important position as a part of the school leadership team, it is incumbent on you to do your part to ensure that the team remains functional at all times, prevent dysfunction within the team, and ensure that staff are unaware of any dysfunction within the team.

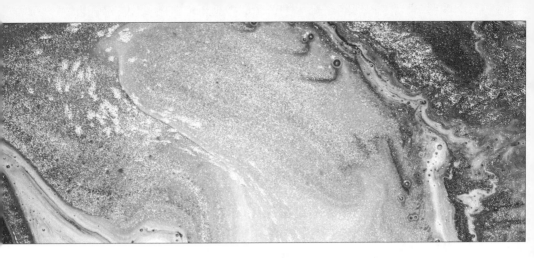

CHAPTER

4

"I'm More Than a Disciplinarian"

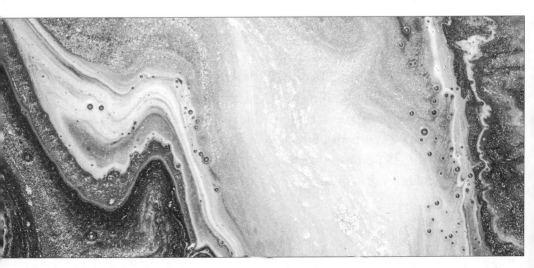

Q18

Do I understand that discipline is not the totality of the assistant principalship?

While I really don't know where the notion of the AP as a school disciplinarian came from, I do know that it is widespread. Also, given the challenges that so many schools face around discipline, I understand why it persists. Somebody must address the discipline issues in the school. But as I stated previously, that shouldn't be an AP—particularly on a full-time basis.

I typically liken discipline to a nice-sized pimple on someone's nose. If the person is self-conscious about their appearance and the perceptions of others relative to how they look, chances are that the pimple is going to be a distraction. So, to either shorten its existence or hide it, the person might apply ointment or makeup, or scratch it, which will prolong its existence. The pimple will, eventually, disappear. The problem, though, is that the pimple will come back. It may not appear in the same place, but it will come back. Why? Because it was never sufficiently dealt with initially. The ointment, makeup, and scratching dealt with the pimple externally—but the problem was *internal*. There's a cause and effect as to why the pimple arose and, until it is addressed internally (such as via diet or stress reduction), it will recur.

I liken behavioral issues in schools to pimples. If undesirable behaviors, issues, and concerns are addressed externally (such as via detentions and suspensions, or worse), the behaviors, issues, and concerns will continually recur. The pimple is a micro issue. The cause of the pimple is a macro issue. Attention must be paid to the macro. Classroom and school discipline issues are micro issues that manifest when the macro—classroom and school climate and culture—either require immediate attention or have become downright toxic and give way to undesirable behaviors. Such behaviors must be addressed. However, rather than doing so via disciplinary referrals and consequences, transform the overall environment in which the students function into one where undesirable behaviors are incompatible with the norms, values, and expectations of the school and have no room to breathe. The focus, then, is on the APs playing their parts in transforming the climate and culture of the school (which we'll discuss in the next question) as opposed to having a good discipline system.

Q19 How does my leadership contribute to a positive school climate and culture?

Of all of the questions in this book, this is probably the most interesting for me and the one on which I will spend the most time.

When I made it public via social media and presentations that I was writing this book, to my surprise, countless teachers reached out to me with strong feelings about what should be included based on their relationships with the APs in their schools. Although they knew nothing about what I would be covering in the book, everyone who contacted me suggested something that be addressed in this question. This spoke volumes to me. In fact, it screamed out to me that, in the minds of the small sampling of teachers who shared their thoughts with me so as to add value to this book, the biggest concern was the interplay between the AP and the overall climate and culture of the school.

In my book *Closing the Attitude Gap: How to Fire Up Your Students to Strive for Success*, I reduced the definitions of climate and culture to one word. I said that climate is simply the "mood" of the school, and that culture is simply the "lifestyle" of the school with the goal of both being to create a schoolwide "mood" and "lifestyle" of excellence. I further went on to say that toward creating this mood and lifestyle of excellence, close examination must be given to the following:

➤ Attitude toward students
➤ Relationship with students
➤ Compassion for students
➤ Environment for learning
➤ Relevance in instruction

As you consider your role and your leadership, and knowing that you are far more than a disciplinarian, how does your leadership contribute to a positive school climate and culture? What is it about your leadership that creates a positive "mood" in the building? Does your leadership lend itself to an environment where students and staff feel welcome? Does your leadership lend itself to an environment where staff want to work and students want to learn? Does your leadership lend itself to an environment where students and staff feel safe emotionally? In other words, does your leadership lend itself to fostering a learning environment that is positive for everyone? Because the entirety of *Closing the Attitude Gap* is devoted to the relationship between staff and students, I want to focus my attention for the remainder of this section on the relationship between the AP and staff.

Communication With Staff

How do you talk to the staff members in the building? What is your tone? What is your temperament? Do you communicate with staff in a way that demonstrates that you respect them as professionals? Do you communicate with staff in a way that demonstrates you appreciate them as professionals? Do you communicate with staff in a way that demonstrates you value them as professionals? Do you welcome staff in the morning with a greeting that conveys that you are glad they are there? All of these things really matter.

You are not going to get the best out of your staff if you do not know how to talk to them. Your communication with your staff is a crucial element to the overall climate and culture of your school. Your communication with your staff must always be professional and courteous. I have observed teachers being addressed rudely, sarcastically, disrespectfully, or as children. While I can certainly relate to the day-to-day frustrations of leadership, we can never lose sight of the goal of a positive school environment, and how you communicate with staff is a key component toward achieving that goal.

What you say and how you say it and your ability and willingness to listen are equally important. You must be a good listener to your staff. If they said it, it's important to them. No matter how busy you are with work, you must always find time to be an attentive listener.

In the context of a positive school climate and culture, I cannot overstate the significance of how staff are welcomed every morning. I am not saying that you must seek them all out and say good morning to them. I am saying, however, that the intentionality of enthusiastically greeting as many teachers as you can every morning goes a long way toward improving the climate, culture, and morale in your school.

Being Approachable to Staff

Closely associated with communicating with staff is being approachable. I vividly recall when, as a brand-new AP, I thought I had to assume a very stereotypical posture of a "tough guy" school administrator. I was aware that a percentage of staff members were intimidated by me (which, in my mind, was a good thing). I had so much to learn! Because some staff were intimidated by me/found me intimidating, I was unapproachable to them. I quickly corrected that flaw (one of many) when I reinvented myself in that school as the principal.

As an AP at your school, relative to the overall climate and culture in your building, you must be approachable. I repeat: you must be approachable! You must be able to position yourself in a way that staff feel comfortable in your presence. Ensure that your presence in the building among staff doesn't create tension, discomfort, and uneasiness. Toward creating a positive school climate and culture, your staff must feel comfortable approaching you and talking to you. This will boil down to your intentionality toward making staff feel comfortable around you, which goes back to how you communicate with your staff.

Follow Up and Follow Through With Staff

Follow through is another important aspect of school culture. You can never afford to make promises and then fail to keep them. Doing so will become your reputation around the building—your brand, your identity. Instead, you want your reputation to be as one who always follows up and follows through on promises made to staff. For example, a teacher having difficulty reaching a parent due to a disconnected home or cell phone number reaches out to you for a solution. If you promised that you would follow up, the teacher now has an expectation that you will, in fact, follow up. If you fail to do so, the teacher may interpret that as her concern not being important to you. If, however, you follow through on your promise in a timely fashion, the teacher can feel confident that you are reliable in situations where administrative support is required, which lends itself favorably to the overall climate and culture of your school.

Being Fair and Consistent With All Staff

As an AP, you can never, ever be perceived as showing favoritism to certain staff members. Trust me, I understand that as human beings it is perfectly normal that we gravitate toward certain people over others—people with whom we have things in common or people with personalities that are compatible with ours, for example. As a school administrator, it is perfectly normal to gravitate toward the teachers who are performing at high levels in their classrooms and whose students have no behavioral issues. However, as an AP, you must be very careful about "normal" tendencies. In other words, the fact that you may appreciate certain staff members a little more because of their work output cannot translate to you treating those staff members more favorably than others. Doing so will undermine your credibility and will adversely affect the climate, culture, and morale of your school. The word will get out that you favor certain teachers over others or that you are fairer with some teachers than others.

> *Case in point—disciplinary referrals:* A teacher was upset with an AP because he felt that the AP didn't handle a student behavioral infraction in a satisfactory manner (as the student was returned to class). The teacher later learned that a student of a colleague's who was sent to the same AP for a behavioral infraction was suspended from school. The teachers were not privy to the nuances of the AP's decision regarding whether to return a student to class or suspend the student; they just knew the outcomes. The implications for you

are with the teacher who's upset and how word spreads throughout the building that you show favoritism to certain teachers and lack consistency. This can undermine your credibility and authority as an AP, adversely affect the school's culture and climate, and kill morale. Therefore, you must always be mindful of how you go about making decisions and, most important, how your decision making is being perceived in the context of being fair and consistent with all staff.

Procedures

As an AP in your school, you get to "see" the school in a way that the average staff member doesn't. Teachers typically have a micro lens through which the bulk of what they see is what goes on in their classrooms. Administrators, however, have a macro lens that enables them to see the entire building. I am certain that, as you see a lot and, based on what you see, there are areas where you feel improvements toward creating a more positive school climate and culture via new or improved existing procedures can and must be made. As many principals afford APs flexibility to enhance school procedures, this is an area where you could potentially have a tremendous impact. The list of areas where new procedures could be introduced or procedural revisions made (we'll explore some of them in Chapter 7) toward an overall smoother operation is infinite. In the meantime, I want you to think about the entire school operation and the way that things are typically done in your school—from how staff and students enter the building in the morning to how staff and students leave the building in the afternoon and everything in between. No procedure will be effective without enforcement and consistency from you, the administrative team, and all building stakeholders. Though you may have developed the best procedures for a school, if those procedures are not enforced to the extent that they become a part of the culture of the school, having developed them was an exercise in futility.

What are some areas that could run more efficiently with new procedures or procedural revisions? In what areas will the principal allow you to make adjustments? Are you proactive in bringing to the attention of the principal those areas that need to be examined procedurally? Remember, the goal is to create as smooth a procedural operation as possible toward enhancing the school's overall climate and culture.

Your Presence

There's a correlation between the message that your presence conveys to your staff and their perception of who and what you represent as the AP at your school. In other words, how you communicate with staff, how approachable you are to staff, your follow up and follow through with staff, how fair and consistent you are with staff, and how you enforce procedures dictate how you are perceived by staff. Your presence speaks volumes. Your presence is your representation of . . . you. You must always be in control of the message your presence conveys to staff. That is, you must consistently ensure that your actions are in line with the message that you intend your presence to convey. The challenge, though, is that you cannot proclaim your presence. Your presence must speak for you. It makes an honest statement to your staff of who you are. It's key that you be in control of your presence in a deliberate effort to communicate effectively, be approachable to staff, follow up and follow through, be fair and consistent with your staff, and enforce procedures. (I will elaborate further on your presence at the end of this chapter.)

Q20 Do I participate in developing staff meeting agendas?

I fully understand that the principal determines whether you are permitted to participate in developing staff meeting agendas. Nevertheless, I ask you to consider this question because if you don't participate in the development of staff meeting agendas, I strongly encourage you to be proactive and let your principal know that you have a wealth of information to share with staff.

The positions of AP and principal are very different and, depending on the leadership style of the principal, can have some degree of overlap. There are aspects of your work as an AP that, though perhaps not on the radar of your principal, are significant and important to the operation of your school. Highlighting your contributions may require that you have input regarding staff meeting agenda items. If you fail to contribute to the agenda, important aspects of the school may be left out and never discussed. I want you to recall what I said about your relationship with your principal and your role toward ensuring that it is productive and try not to avoid having a conversation about your role in assisting with the agenda. Because the principal doesn't have your eyes and ears and won't see what you see or hear what you hear, your input in meeting agendas is vital toward keeping staff fully informed and increasing the probability that all issues and concerns are addressed.

Q21 Do I engage staff during staff meetings?

This question is closely related to the previous one. Do you engage staff during staff meetings? As I recall, during my days as an AP, my participation in staff meetings was minimal to nonexistent. As a result of the leadership style of the principal, I wasn't permitted to say much of anything in staff meetings. It was the principal's show. But I used that reality as a real-time graduate school course and learned what not to do when I one day became a principal. I knew that my principal's approach was problematic and that staff were being deprived of vital information. Although I was serving as a full-time disciplinarian, I had information to share with staff. While I couldn't consistently get information to staff collectively, I made sure that I got it to them individually. The school would have been so much more efficient had I been able to engage with staff during staff meetings.

Are you permitted to participate in staff meetings in your capacity as assistant principal? What types of items are you permitted to address? Are you able to be a part of the discussion on teaching and learning? As one of the leaders in your school, it is imperative that you are viewed as someone important, as one who has much to contribute to the success of the school, and as an educator. As long as you are seen as, for example, a full-time disciplinarian, it will be very difficult for staff to take you seriously as an educator or instructional leader (in the truest senses of what it means to be an educator and instructional leader). As the chapter title states, you are more than a disciplinarian.

Q22 Do I attend PTO/PTA meetings?

I don't recall ever missing a PTA/PTO meeting (unless I was ill or out of town on school business) as an AP or principal. I felt that, as a leader, the only place for me to be when there was a PTA/PTO meeting was . . . at the PTA/PTO meeting. Why? Because they were important parent-led meetings. Although the meetings were not consistently well attended, there were always enough parents present for them to be productive.

I was not directly involved in those meetings as an AP or a principal, and neither should you. Those are not your meetings. These are meetings led by officers elected by parents. I regularly attended the meetings for two reasons—I wanted to be informed, and I wanted parents to know that I cared about what mattered to them. As a leader, I wanted to be informed and armed with as much information about parents' concerns and parental decision making as possible. In well-functioning PTAs/PTOs, there is a great deal of invaluable information being shared and exchanged and, as an administrator, I wanted to be on top of it.

Attending those meetings to demonstrate to parents that they mattered and that I cared about the things that mattered to them made for long days (as PTA/PTO meetings typically began at 7:00 pm). But as a result of attending those meetings, I was much farther "ahead of the curve" than the leaders who didn't attend them. I was informed and demonstrated my interest via my presence. As a school leader, why wouldn't I have wanted to attend meetings of my students' parents?

As both an AP and principal, I was commonly asked by the PTA/PTO president to make opening remarks (typically a summary of the state of the school). I welcomed this opportunity and kept my remarks brief. I also welcomed the opportunity to engage in Q&As with parents, as it allowed me to share pertinent information with them.

Does your school have a PTA/PTO? Are PTA/PTO meetings held regularly? Are the meetings well attended? In your capacity as assistant principal, do you regularly attend your school's PTA/PTO meetings? If not, why not? If so, why do you attend the meetings? Are the meetings beneficial for your school and students? These are important questions because the fact that PTAs/PTOs are parent-led and organized doesn't exclude you from participation in them. If PTOs/PTAs don't exist or are low-functioning, your input toward establishing them or improving their function is necessary.

I strongly recommend that you make yourself a fixture in your school's PTA/PTO meetings—if your principal approves of your attending them. As an AP who aspires to be a principal, there is a lot to know in your capacity as a leader. Part of your expertise must be parent concerns and the PTA/PTO meetings are forums where those concerns will be brought to light. If you don't attend the meetings, you will miss out on valuable information that will likely have implications for the operation of your school.

Q23 Do I attend school board meetings?

When I was a classroom teacher hungry to become a principal, one of my graduate school professors told the class that we needed to attend our local school board meetings. He told us that those meetings were where the business of the district took place and that we needed to develop an understanding of how the district conducted its business. Although I wasn't eager to add yet another new dimension to my already packed and challenging schedule, I was so "hungry" to become a school administrator that I heeded his advice and attended every school board meeting during my six years in a particular district—as a 5th grade teacher, as an AP, and as a principal (at which level my principal colleagues and I were expected attend). Attendance was taken by one of the assistant superintendents! Our district expected us to attend all board meetings both because the business of the district was taking place in real time and because, on any given evening, a parent, student, or community member could raise a concern to which we (as opposed to the superintendent) were to respond.

I eventually left that district and moved to one where, to my surprise, principals were not encouraged to attend, and didn't attend, school board meetings. I wondered why principal attendance at board meetings wasn't expected, why principals didn't want to attend board meetings, and why senior administration wouldn't want principals to respond to parent, student, and community concerns.

While I understand that no two districts are alike and that districts do things a certain way for very specific reasons, I strongly recommend that you regularly attend school board meetings. As you are preparing to one day being principal, you must be well versed on how your school district conducts its business—a vital area of school leadership. If, by chance, building-level administrators are discouraged (for whatever reason) from attending school board meetings, attend your local school board meetings instead. Learn how boards of education function within your local school board. If you reside in the district in which you work, attend school board meetings as a local resident. The bottom line is that you must attend school board meetings somewhere, and preferably in the district in which you serve as an assistant principal.

Q24 How do I maximize parental engagement?

Predicated on the way that APs are typically utilized, you have access to a plethora of parents. If you have, in fact, been relegated to the role of full-time disciplinarian, look at the glass as half full as opposed to half empty because your access to parents can be a win for the entire school community. For example, in schools and districts where large volumes of disciplinary referrals are typically generated daily, phone calls home need not be solely devoted to reporting disciplinary infractions; they can be used to engage parents in constructive and productive conversations. Instead of reacting to situations as they arise, you can periodically call the parents of students who have exhibited undesirable behaviors to check in and follow up on strategies that may have been suggested during a prior conversation. What's key is that you proactively maximize parental engagement. You'll want to put yourself in a position to establish credibility in the eyes of parents.

Looking at parental engagement at the building level, outside of the PTA/PTO structure, there are countless ways that your school can be an asset to your students' parents and families (e.g., via programs that provide a variety of strategies of support). Putting the programs together, however, is not the challenge. The challenge is getting the parents into the building, and key to getting them into the school is the overall health of the culture of the school. Is the culture of your school healthy? Is the culture of your school inclusive of parental engagement? Is the culture of your school welcoming to parents? Is the culture of your school conducive to high levels of parental engagement? Parents must *want* to be in your building, and how you interact with them will go a long way toward sustaining their engagement. In many cases, the AP is the initial point of contact with parents at the building level. That contact must be positive if you are going to effectively engage the mass of parents. As you successfully engage in positive dialogue with and create a culture of positive dialogue for parents, you are essentially creating a culture of parental inclusion that will lend itself to maximizing parents' engagement in your school.

Students' arrival and dismissal times are golden opportunities to quickly forge positive relations with parents. By being outside during student arrival and dismissal, you can greet parents with a friendly "Good morning" or "Good afternoon" when they drop off and pick up their children—a win for everyone. (A lengthy conversation is only required if you or the parent has a need for one.) Your objective is simply to demonstrate your presence and visibility and exchange pleasantries with parents (as opposed to communicating with parents only when there are problems). You are developing a rapport with parents, which puts you in a better position to engage parents in brief conversations about upcoming events involving them.

Q25 How do I maximize community engagement?

School leadership is not an easy endeavor. Quite frankly, it isn't for everyone. It takes a very special individual to endure the enormous challenges of the assistant principalship. I know for a fact that there are plenty of principals who are much more effective as principals than they were as APs. I have nothing but respect for the countless APs who work to make teachers better and lift students to higher heights.

School leaders must always remember that their schools are not islands. Your schools are in cities and towns surrounded by a wealth of human resources. As difficult and challenging as the work may be, there are people from all walks of life who would love to take it on and work with your school. The human capital that surrounds your school could be a tremendous asset to your school. You just have to tap into who and what's out there.

> *Case in point:* As a new principal, I inherited a school with very low state assessment scores that needed to be improved . . . yesterday! There was a great deal of pressure on me to deliver. Toward addressing the issue, we tapped approximately 20 retired teachers from the community and asked them to spend two semesters assisting students in math and reading before the state assessments in the winter. That proved to be an invaluable strategy, and the value of those retired teachers was immeasurable. To benefit the school and students,

instead of trying to do everything ourselves, we tapped into the resources of the community.

We started a Young Men's Empowerment Program (about which I wrote extensively in my book *Motivating Black Males to Achieve in School & in Life*). For that program to work, I needed the support of men in the community. I was able to tap more than 100 men from all walks of life to volunteer to be a part of the empowerment of our young men. And for our Young Women's Empowerment Program, we tapped and asked to serve as volunteers women from the community.

In what ways have you tapped into the human capital surrounding your school? Have you made the community aware that you'd like to partner with it in various capacities? Have you and your administrative team identified ways that community members can be assets to your school? The foregoing are examples of ways that APs can play a role in initiating tapping into community resources. While in most cases community members are eager to work with schools on a volunteer basis, they are not going to make the initial contact. That's where you come in. You can partner with your principal and administrative team to identify your school's needs, determine the role the community can play toward meeting the needs, and formulate a course of action. Your school doesn't have to be an island.

Q26 Do I maintain a presence that speaks to how I want to be perceived by my students and staff?

As I close out this chapter, entitled, "I'm More Than a Disciplinarian," let me remind you that, as an AP, you *are* more than a disciplinarian. You are one of the leaders of your school. It is my hope that this and the other chapters of this book have made it very clear to you that discipline is only a small portion of what you should be doing in your school. As the culminating question of this chapter, then, I ask you, do you maintain a presence in your school that speaks to how you want to be perceived by your students and staff? What message does your presence convey to your students? What message does your presence convey to your staff? Always know that your presence—not just what you say and do—in your school speaks to how you are perceived. Although what you say and do contribute to your overall presence in the building, how you are perceived by students and staff is the more accurate account of who you are in their eyes. For example, if students and staff seldom see you, your absence defines your presence. If students solely see you in your role as disciplinarian, then that's who you are in their eyes.

I am going to assume that, like myself, you want to be perceived as an educator in the truest sense of the word. If that is the case, you must position yourself as an educator. That is, you must be present as an educator and do the things that educators do. You must be a master of shaping your own presence to the extent that it is consistent with how you are perceived. If you talk about education without functioning as an educator, you are simply who all perceive you to be—and that could be a problem.

As I shared earlier, as an AP, I functioned as a disciplinarian, a cafeteria duty supervisor, and a teacher supply inventory clerk. Serving in those capacities shaped how I was perceived by students and staff. Because of the significance that education held in my life, I had an innate need to change the way I was perceived by students and staff. With the permission of the principal of the middle school where I served as AP, I was able to introduce academic programs such as Battle of the Homerooms—a schoolwide trivia competition in which Black History questions were posed during the morning announcements throughout the month of February. In Battle, each homeroom class was responsible for coming up with an answer and one representative per homeroom would place the answer in a box in my office following the morning announcements. At the end of the month, the top two homerooms in each grade squared off in a schoolwide assembly that I moderated. The six homeroom classes were represented by six students chosen by the students in the homeroom classes. The winning team received trophies and the students in the winning homerooms were awarded with a pizza party. Battle of the Homerooms became a huge hit in the school. Because the entire school knew that it was my "baby," the perception of who and what I was changed completely. I, too, was perceived as an educator because I positioned myself to be perceived as one. The new way in which I was perceived carried into my principalship (as I soon after became principal of the school and Battle of the Homerooms competitions were held throughout the year).

As an AP in your school, you, too, must be ever so conscious of what your presence in your school means to students and staff and how you are perceived. It truly matters.

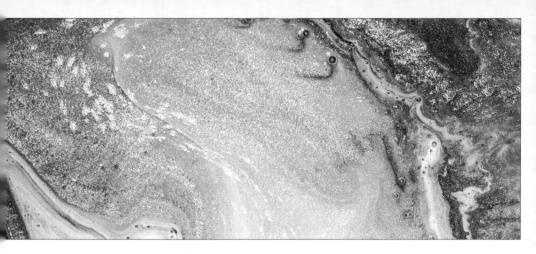

CHAPTER

5

There's Much to Know as an Assistant Principal

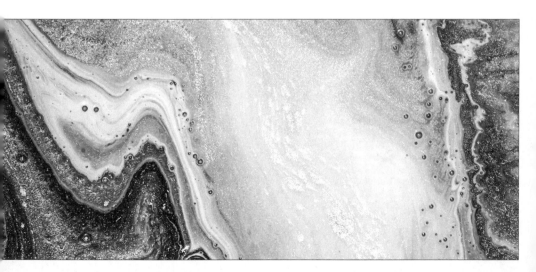

As the chapter title states, there's much to know as an AP. On the one hand, there's the day-to-day work about which you must be knowledgeable and proficient in carrying out. On the other hand, there are the things that may not be directly related to your role as an AP with which you must be familiar—particularly if you aspire to become a principal. As I stated previously, much of what you are exposed to will boil down to your principal's willingness to involve you in the fullness of school leadership while you serve as an AP. But let's say you are not being exposed to the breadth and depth of school leadership, for whatever reason; that shouldn't prevent you from seeking knowledge and information on your own. In this chapter, I will cover school district policies, state statutes and codes, special education law, teachers' union contracts, support staff union contracts, district curriculum, state content standards, and the school budget—all of which you can learn about on your own.

During my administrative internship, my mentor, Dr. Kenneth King, required that I be well versed in the areas that I will cover in this chapter—long before I became an assistant principal. For the purposes of this book, I strongly recommend that you do the same.

Q27 Am I conversant in my school district's policies?

Are you conversant in your school district's policies? I'm not asking if you're *familiar* with your school district's policies (which is not good enough and can get you into a lot of trouble) but if you are *conversant* in them. I'm asking you if you know them as if you wrote them. You've got to know them *thoroughly*. This means that you must, if you haven't already, gain access to your district's policies and *read* and *study* them. In your capacity as AP, you make numerous split-second decisions. Your decisions cannot be emotional ones (as decisions based on emotion can come back to haunt you). Your decision making must be rooted and grounded in your district's policies (and the law, which we will get to). If you are making decisions that contradict your district's policies, in an extreme case, your career as a school administrator may be jeopardized. As I stated previously numerous times, many APs spend an inordinate amount of their time disciplining students. Well, the consequences that you impose must be grounded in district policy. You can't, based on emotion, suspend a student for however many days you may deem fit if your district's policy doesn't support your actions. Ignorance of the policies is never a valid excuse.

Are you conversant in your school district's policies? Do you review them regularly? Is your decision making grounded in your school district's policies? Know your school district's policies. Obtain your own copies and keep them close by. Reference them frequently. The information is vital.

Q28 Am I conversant in my state's statutes and codes?

Closely associated with your district's policies are your state's education laws in the form of statutes and codes. Hear me well, AP: *You are not equipped to lead if you do not know education law!* Plain and simple. Regardless of how great a leader you are, if you do not know the law, you could prove to be a liability to your school. As I stated previously, you cannot make decisions based on emotions. As your decisions could have legal implications, they must be supported by education law.

During my administrative internship, my mentor brought the New Jersey State Statute books to me at the school where I was teaching and told me that I had to learn the laws. The books were thick and the print was small. As a 5th grade teacher who aspired to be an AP, the books seemed awfully intimidating. However, over time, I settled into them and, as a result, was prepared to lead when the time came. Are you conversant in your state's statutes and codes? Do you review them regularly? Are your decisions supported by education law? Be sure to keep a copy of your state's statutes and codes close by and take the time necessary to get to know the education laws of your state thoroughly.

Q 29 Am I conversant in special education law?

I purposely created a question about special education law because of its significance. I cannot overemphasize how important it is that you are well versed in special education law. Ignorance of special education law can be a career-ender and can never be offered as an excuse. Special education law is extremely complex and there is a ton to know and learn—both on the federal and state sides. As with your school district's policies, obtain copies of both federal and state special education law and take the time necessary to know and become conversant in both.

Q 30 Am I conversant in our teachers' union contract?

My days as an administrative intern were extremely rewarding and prepared me for the assistant principalship and the principalship. Because teachers' contracts were not discussed in my graduate school courses, I never gave them a second thought. However, they became a major topic of discussion during my internship (perhaps a given when your mentor is the assistant superintendent for human resources). He stressed how important it was that I know the teacher's contract backwards, forwards, inside, and out and that, when making decisions, I know the teachers' rights—which proved invaluable toward my effectiveness as an AP and as a principal. I spent many evenings studying the teachers' contract. Taking pride in knowing the contract as if I had been a teacher prevented me from unintentionally violating teachers' rights. For those of you who work in unionized districts, how conversant are you in your teachers' contract? How often do you refer to it? When last did you look at it? As the title of this chapter states, there's much to know as an AP, which includes knowledge of contracts— teacher's contracts *and* support staff contracts.

Q31 Am I conversant in our support staff union contract?

If you are working in a unionized school district, chances are the teachers are not the only employee group represented by a union. Every employee in your building may be represented by a bargaining unit. Therefore, they will have contracts and, as an administrator in your building, you must be conversant in the contracts of *all* employees. Staff have rights as employees and, as one of the administrators in your building, you must know those rights. This will require that you spend time learning the contracts of all the employee groups represented in your school to ensure that your decisions and actions in your capacity as AP never violate the rights of the employees who work in your building.

Q32 Am I conversant in our district's curriculum and state content standards?

As I organized this book, I vacillated as to whether to include this question in the chapter on instructional leadership (Chapter 2) or in this chapter. I finally decided to include it here. Children are in school to learn. Student achievement is the goal and all else that we do (e.g., the various programs we institute to support student learning) serve as the vehicles to get there.

Your school's curriculum (along with great teachers) is the lifeblood of student achievement. Everything that your students are expected to know and do comes from your school and district curricula. As a school administrator, an AP in this case, your expertise in curriculum is not optional. In your capacity as an instructional leader and educator in your building, you must be conversant in curriculum. Imagine, if you will, you are in a classroom observing instruction and you are unfamiliar with the curriculum. My question for you then would be, what exactly are you observing? In other words, how would you be able to gauge whether what was being taught was that expected by the district if you lack knowledge of district curricula? The answer is, you wouldn't, and the students would suffer as a result.

You must be as conversant in your state's content standards as you are in your district's curricula. For the past two decades, more pressure has been put on districts, schools, staff, and students to have students pass state standardized assessments than ever before in the history of American education—particularly in schools and districts situated in low socioeconomic communities. As a school leader and AP, you can never succumb to the pressure of requiring teachers to teach to a test to raise assessment scores. Teaching to a test is not quality education; it's rote memorization that typically lasts until the assessment is over. You must become an expert in your district's curricula and your state's content standards and hold the teachers who you supervise accountable for teaching not to a test but to your district's curricula and your state's content standards. Is this easy? Not at all, but it is vital. The starting point is your expertise in curriculum and standards. How conversant are you in your district's curriculum and state content standards? What role do they play toward your overall supervision of teachers? What role do they play toward student achievement in your school? The answers to these questions are vital to the goal of student achievement in your school.

Q33 Am I conversant in our school's budget?

If the curriculum (along with great teachers) is the lifeblood of student achievement, then the school budget is the lifeblood of the entire school operation. Everything in a school costs money and whether there will be money to pay for the various programs is contingent on how a budget is managed and balanced. As an AP, as I have stated several times in this book, what you are exposed to is, in large part, predicated on what your principal allows you to be exposed to. In an ideal situation, the principal is committed to your leadership development and exposing you to how to build, manage, and balance a budget is a no-brainer. However, in a situation where an AP has been relegated to serving as a full-time disciplinarian, chances are good that she will never or rarely see a school budget, knowledge of which is a crucial component to AP development toward becoming a principal.

Are you conversant in your school's budget? Are you exposed to your school's budget? Do you play a role in managing your school's budget? Do you personally do any spending from your school's budget? Always remember that there is a direct correlation between how money is allocated and spent and what happens in classrooms with children. If you are not exposed to your school's budget (and didn't learn about budgets in graduate school), it behooves you to stretch yourself and take the initiative to learn the principles of building, managing, and balancing a budget outside of your school. You can readily access information about budgets online or through other administrators. You simply have to take the initiative because, when you one day become a principal, you have to be able to hit the ground running.

Q34 Am I an active participant in school-level planning?

This is actually a very important question. School-level planning is vital to the progress of a school. School-level planning teams typically comprise the principal, other administrators (not necessarily all), a sampling of teachers and various other support staff, parents, students, and members of the community. As an AP, being a member of the school-level planning team is a good opportunity (particularly if you are an aspiring principal) because it gives you a voice in the overall planning of the school. One of the ways that APs are utilized by their principals is as members of school-level planning teams. Because as an AP I was not selected to be a member of the school-level planning team, I kept abreast of the team's agenda and activities. If you are given the opportunity to serve on the school-level planning team, I strongly encourage you to take it.

Q35 Is all that I do and all that I know preparing me for the principalship?

As the title of this chapter states, there's much to know as an assistant principal. I have detailed several important areas about which an AP needs to know in this and previous chapters. The learning *never* ends. Even if your role is limited, there's still always *something* new to learn every day. You are learning from your principal, other administrators, staff, parents, students, and members of the community. You are also learning while doing. Each day brings new and different challenges that, along with the demands of your work, engender a tremendous amount of new learning throughout the course of any given day. But again, the degree to which your principal exposes you to various facets of leadership will dictate how much you are able to learn during your tenure as an AP.

As an AP, you must never lose sight of the fact that your professional learning can never be limited to the graduate program you completed or the work you do on the job. It is imperative that you always seek out opportunities for professional learning. You must be obsessed with obtaining new information via books, journals, articles, blog posts, online education content, PLNs via social media, conferences, institutes, in-services, networking with colleagues, and thought partnerships with peers. Professional learning opportunities are infinite; you just have to take advantage of them. You must be highly intentional about consistently growing as a school leader. Therefore, professional learning must be a routine aspect of your AP repertoire toward either being the most effective AP you can be or preparing to be the principal of your own school.

Are you an aspiring principal? Do you desire to one day lead your own school? Do you envision taking a school to heights previously unimagined? Is the principalship your dream? Or, are you content with your assistant principalship and, therefore, have no desire to lead your own school as a principal? Are you interested in one day transitioning into another administrative position, such as a central office position rather than the principalship? In my capacity as an education consultant, I am typically and frequently asked (in person and via e-mails and DMs from APs from all over the United States), "When do you think one is ready to start applying for the principalship?" This question usually leads to discussions/communications about preparation for the next level. Some individuals are very prepared, while others (like me when I was an AP) are not. My response, though, is quite simple—you are ready to start applying for a position at the next level when you *feel* that you are ready. It's what you *feel* within yourself.

As an AP, you could be in the most ideal situation—being your principal's right arm—and, therefore, fully engaged in all aspects of school leadership. While this has theoretically prepared you for the next level, it still boils down to what you *feel*. In addition to, ideally, being fully prepared for the next level in terms of exposure to the various aspects of leadership, you must be emotionally prepared for the principalship—a totally different world than the assistant principalship. While your principal may fully expose you to facets of leadership, the reality is that the buck doesn't stop with you. You are not held accountable by the superintendent of schools. The buck stops with the principal, and it is she who is held accountable by the superintendent. The principal is held accountable for decisions *you* make and the actions *you* take. If you make an egregious error, chances are that the principal is going to be held accountable by the superintendent because, as AP, you are an extension of the principal. Again, your role as an AP is to assist the principal. As a principal, you must be emotionally prepared for the level of accountability that comes with the position.

I served as an AP for a year and a half. As I stated, my exposure to school leadership was quite limited. But by the end of six months, I was, in my mind, fully prepared for the principalship. That is, although I knew very little, emotionally I felt strongly that I could step into the role of principal and perform at a high level. I was convinced that I could teach myself everything that I didn't learn as an AP. My point here is that readiness for the principalship is personal and predicated on the individual. Some may never be ready. It's a very demanding, fast-paced position that can consume anywhere from 10 to 14 hours of your day, and weekends; that isn't for everyone. Although you could be fully exposed to the various facets of leadership and all that you know and do are preparing you for leadership, the demands that the principalship makes on your time may lead you to determine that it isn't for you—at this time. The decision to pursue the principalship is a very personal one and will require that you weigh the pros and cons of all aspects, including time, of the position. If after doing so you feel that the principalship is, in fact, for you, then as far as I am concerned, the time to start pursuing the position is ... now.

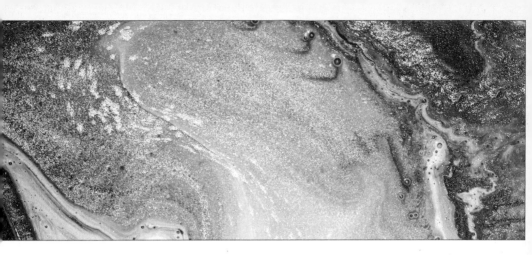

CHAPTER

6

Engagement Comes Before Achievement!

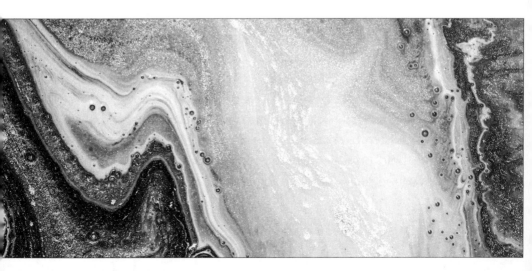

Q36 Do I attend extracurricular activities and events?

This was one of those areas during my days as an AP where I could do what I wanted. As the AP, I had a stake in the success of the students. Therefore, I attended every event during that year and a half. I wanted to both see my students in their respective extracurricular capacities and have the students see that I was interested in them outside of the classroom. I knew that showing interest in my students outside of the course of the school day would go a long way toward developing solid relationships with them. I made attendance at their various extracurricular activities a priority.

When I much later became a high school principal, I maintained the practice of attending students' extracurricular activities and events. The sport that will always stand out for me is soccer. As a principal of a school with a varsity program, I inherited a soccer program. I do not like soccer. I do not understand soccer. I have no interest in soccer. But as the principal of a school with a soccer program, I attended both home and away soccer games. That's right. I attended the games—even a long state tournament game held on a cold, rainy, and windy Friday afternoon (the young men, happy to see me, yelled, "Mr. Kafele, Mr.

Kafele" when I arrived; my presence made their day)—to support my students.

How often do you attend extracurricular activities inside and outside of your school? Is attendance at student activities part of your leadership repertoire? Are your students happy to see you when you attend the events? In your capacity as AP, I implore you to attend as many extracurricular activities and events as you can. Your students are counting on your presence. As the title of this chapter states, engagement comes before achievement. Because many young people do not have parental support in the stands, you can serve as students' support. You are that engagement. You are significant in their lives. You are somebody special to them. You matter. Yes, it will require that you spend more time at school/away from home and sometimes give up weekends. But always know what your presence at your students' extracurricular events means to both the students participating and those there to support their classmates. Your presence speaks volumes to all.

Q37 Do I engage with students beyond my disciplinary and supervisory roles?

As an AP, I had one nonnegotiable—a guiding principle, if you will: student engagement. I felt strongly that it was important to daily have solid interactions with students about anything under the sun. It was important to me to have conversations with students about things that were meaningful to them, not just school-related conversations.

Those conversations could occur in the hallways between classes, in the cafeteria during lunch, or outside before or after school. The bottom line was engaging students in healthy, meaningful conversations. This enabled students to get to know me as someone other than the Assistant Principal and allowed me to get to know the students outside of their academic capacities.

How often do you engage with your students outside of your disciplinary and supervisory capacities? What types of conversations are you able to have with your students? Do your students seem genuinely interested in having conversations with you? If you find that your conversations with students typically center around discipline, I strongly encourage you to get to know your students on another level by having conversations with them throughout the day about topics other than behavior.

> *Case in point:* During the first week of my assistant principalship at a middle school, one of the things that stood out for me about the physical building was that it had no "life." Other than a mural, there was nothing on the walls that "spoke" to the students. Given the OK by the principal to hang motivational quotes and posters of historical figures that were representative of our student body on the walls all over the building, I spent an entire evening hanging quotes and posters on every hallway wall, in stairwells, in the cafeteria, in the main office, and in my office. When the students arrived the following morning, they

were shocked by the new look of the school. What they didn't realize was that the walls would become my vehicles for student engagement. The walls became my classroom. As students changed classes each period, instead of me saying "Hello" and telling them to keep it moving, I could now stop groups of students and draw their attention to a quote or poster and engage them in conversations about what they read or saw. I had very powerful hallway conversations with students and engaged them on a variety of topics.

As engagement comes before achievement, I strongly encourage you to keep your students engaged. Try what I did with the quotes and posters (if your principal approves) or look into other strategies to engage your students, and sustain healthy engagement with them.

Q38 What do my mornings look like during student arrival and my afternoons look like immediately following the dismissal bell?

This question addresses one of my biggest pet peeves in school leadership (as those of you who have heard me present are well aware). I strongly believe that during the hour that students are arriving at school and the hour that students are being dismissed, there is only one place on the planet for the school leadership to be: outside with the students. Neither is the time for anything other than greeting students (as they arrive in the morning) and seeing students off (as they leave to go home).

During workshops, this is typically a topic that I discuss with principals. I remind them that, despite their workloads, they have to be present during student arrival and dismissal. For the purpose of this book and in your role as AP, I am saying emphatically that the same holds true for you. It may be a bit tricky, though, as you are an *assistant* principal and not the principal. If the principal decides to utilize you differently during student arrival and dismissal, then you have no choice but to comply (because you are in your building to assist your principal).

With regard to the question at hand, let's assume that your principal gives you the green light to be outdoors during student arrival and dismissal. You must seize the opportunity. During arrival, your presence lays a foundation and sets a tone for the remainder of the day. It allows you to look into the eyes of every student as they arrive (which is significant as students' eyes are their "newspapers"). For example, if a student is dealing with something heavy, you will likely be able to detect that in her eyes. If you are not able to look into students' eyes, you may miss some very important information about them. Your presence in the morning allows you to personalize welcoming students into the building. It allows you to greet students by name, shake their hands or give them a high-five, and let them know that you are excited to see them. Your presence in the morning provides parents with a sense of security (as they know that their children are in good hands because a school leader is outside greeting them). I can't emphasize enough the power of the presence of members of the leadership team greeting the students in the morning. One caveat that must be taken seriously is this: your presence has to matter to your students. Your presence has to mean something to your students. You have to be perceived by your students as someone credible in their lives—someone who matters, someone they trust, someone they respect. If your presence fails to matter to students, everything mentioned previously is for naught.

The presence of a school leader during after-school dismissal is as important as having such a presence during student arrival in the mornings. Your presence in the afternoon will give students who need to but were unable to speak with you during the day an opportunity to do so. Likewise, your presence in the afternoon affords you an opportunity to reach out to students who you may not have had an opportunity to speak to during the day. Your presence in the afternoon allows you to monitor the movement of your students as they leave the school grounds, and parents will know that their children are in good hands.

Are you present at the entrance of your school during student arrival? Are you present at the entrance of your school during student dismissal? If not, why not? If so, to what extent is your presence beneficial to your students? Again, if you are in a situation where your principal permits you to greet your students in the morning and see your students off in the afternoon—important parts of the day for students—seize the opportunity.

Q39 What programs, clubs, or activities have I instituted at my school?

As an AP, while there was much that I wanted to do in my new school, I clearly understood my role and my "lane." Some initiatives that I suggested as an AP were instituted during my assistant principalship and some were instituted when I became principal of the same building.

I developed a profound interest in African American history as an undergraduate. I grew up in a predominantly African American city in New Jersey and attended predominantly African American schools. When I decided to become a teacher, I returned to the school district where I was a student and subsequently became an AP and principal in that district. I knew instinctively that because African American history was significant in my life and to my trajectory as a professional and as a man, there was a place for it in my school. For 10 years of my life (from the ages of 13 to 23), I did absolutely nothing to enhance my life. That decade, which included five years of high school and having a cumulative GPA of 1.5, was difficult and challenging. After I graduated from high school, I was in and out of junior college for the next five years (as I was repeatedly placed on academic probation for showing up but doing absolutely nothing). My love in life was everything the streets had to offer at that time. At the age of 23, in an effort to do something productive with my life, I enrolled at Kean University in New Jersey and graduated two years later—summa cum laude. What accounted for the drastic turn of events? On my very first day of classes at Kean, I stumbled upon African American history—which introduced me to myself beyond the name on my birth certificate. I read voraciously for the first time in my life and, in the process, discovered who I was historically. My academic course work became very easy for me because I knew who I was historically. I knew that I was a descendent of greatness and understood my role along the continuum.

The preceding paragraph relates to this question because I knew as an AP that there was a place (and a need) for African American history in my school. Although I knew of its ability to transform, there were no courses for it outside of the social studies curriculum. I pondered how I could expose my students to this information until it hit me! I decided that instead of having the students sit in the cafeteria doing nothing during the four-hour detention that I was assigned to monitor on Saturdays, I would turn detention into an African American history class. Well, predictably, the word got out to the parents and it seemed like practically all of them wanted their children to learn African American history with me on Saturday mornings. Because the initial intent of detention was lost, I changed the name to the Saturday Morning African American History Institute. Students who warranted detention were assigned to it, but the information the students attained was so valuable that it served as a deterrent to many of the behaviors that sent them there. Having my Saturday morning detention morph into the African American Institute enabled me to engage students in ways that otherwise wouldn't have been possible. The Institute, a big hit at my school, served as the impetus for a magnet program I created two years later under my principalship, during which time the school became the Sojourner Truth Middle School Institute of Science, Technology, and African-Centered Studies.

In your capacity as assistant principal, what programs, clubs, or activities have you instituted at your school? Has your principal given you the latitude to launch a program, club, or activity? Have you worked with other staff toward the creation of new programs, clubs, or activities? Remember, engagement comes before achievement, so the more ways you have to engage students, the higher the probability that intended student academic outcomes will be achieved.

Q40 What is my overall worth to my students?

As I close out this chapter, I bring your attention to its title—Engagement Comes Before Achievement. As I've stated throughout the chapter, your engagement of students is vital. To that end, What is your worth to your students? What is your value to your students? Are your students better because you are an assistant principal in your school? Are your students at an advantage because of your presence in your school? Would your students' degree of success be higher if someone else was in your role? Are you, in your capacity as assistant principal, an asset to your students? These are critical questions that I challenge you to ask yourself regularly, if not daily. Yes, there's always a possibility that answering truthfully may hurt; that simply

means that you have work to do because, at the proverbial end of the day, your worth to your students must be
immeasurable.

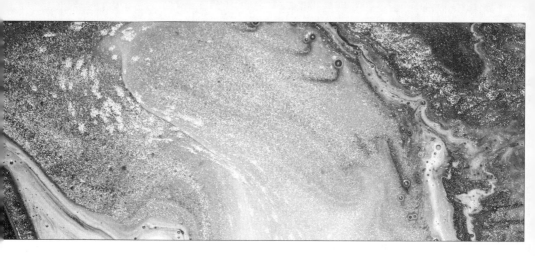

CHAPTER

7

. . . .

Procedures Equal Progress

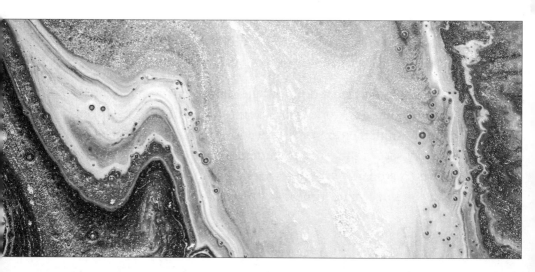

Throughout this book, I have talked about the role of the AP relative to what an AP is ideally—an instructional leader—to what an AP actually is in far too many instances—a full-time disciplinarian. This chapter's focus is on procedures that fall within the realm of the responsibilities of the AP.

Q41 Following my assessment of my school, what student and staff procedures have I recommended to the principal?

As important as instructional leadership, teaching, learning, and achievement are, they must all take place in a school whose culture allows instructional leadership, teaching, learning, and achievement to occur at optimal levels. A part of this culture are the procedures in place to meet certain movement objectives at the building and classroom levels. As you walk through your building with eyes and ears wide open, what procedures relative to movement will you recommend be implemented? What procedures relative to movement will you recommend be revised?

For example, depending on the dynamics of your school, a procedure for student arrival into the building may need to be implemented or a procedure in place may need to be revised. Is the current student arrival procedure conducive to students arriving at school and at their classes in an organized and timely fashion? Does it minimize hall and stairwell traffic and congestion? Does it incorporate staff assisting students? Or, at the secondary level, what procedures aimed at ensuring that students arrive at their next class within the expected time frame are in place? Or during a fire drill, what procedures for ensuring that all students and staff are able to evacuate the building quickly, quietly, and in an orderly fashion within the expected time frame are in place? In your capacity as AP, building procedures are typically, but not necessarily exclusively, among your responsibilities. It behooves you, then, to learn and know all aspects of your school procedurally so that you are in better position to make solid recommendations to your principal about procedures.

Regarding staff, what procedures lend themselves to a smoother overall operation? For example, what are the parking procedures? In some schools, this is an enormous challenge for administration in general and the AP specifically (as, for example, a situation wherein some teachers have choice parking spaces and others have a long walk to the building can adversely affect morale). As an AP, it becomes your responsibility to devise a parking procedure that keeps everyone happy. Another staff procedure that may require your attention is the staff sign-in procedure. It is not uncommon for some teachers to run late and bypass signing in (so that they can get to their classrooms quickly). If those teachers neglect to sign in when they get a free moment as intended, officially there is no documented proof of if and when they reported to work. What procedure would you put in place to ensure that all teachers are accounted for regardless of challenges in the morning?

Let's look at a few other areas that typically fall under the purview of the AP.

Q42 If cafeteria duty is my responsibility, what procedures have I put in place to ensure smooth transitions to and from the cafeteria?

I can still vividly recall my first day as a new AP more than 20 years ago: getting up early in the morning, mentally preparing for my new endeavor, walking the halls, receiving advice from supporters, and so much more. But what stands out to me most on that first day was what occurred while I was on cafeteria duty (my baptism into my assistant principalship, as it were): as I circulated the cafeteria to learn the landscape, I suddenly had to break up a fight between two 7th grade male students. I knew then and there that I had to put in place procedures to prevent the recurrence of physical altercations between students. As I assessed the state of the cafeteria, I saw that it lacked structure and that student movement was a bit too free. After the cafeteria was reorganized, restructured, and made more manageable, no other fights occurred in the cafeteria during my 14-year tenure as a school leader in four buildings.

I am certain that many APs who will read this book are responsible for cafeteria duty. In my role as a consultant, I have visited countless school cafeterias during lunch periods. The moment I enter a cafeteria, I can detect whether it requires attention relative to procedures (if not before I enter via the volume of noise and students who are in hallways instead of in the cafeteria). When responsible for cafeteria duty, you can never lose sight of the fact that structure, order, and procedures are for the sake of a smooth-running cafeteria and how students will arrive at their classes immediately following the lunch period. As well, how students arrive at the cafeteria from their classes must be considered. As I've observed over the years, the transition from class to the cafeteria can be challenging in some schools. As you envision your procedures for the lunch periods, you must also consider how students transition to the cafeteria; how students enter the cafeteria; how students interact while in the cafeteria; the effect that students who arrive late have on the flow of the cafeteria; how students exit the cafeteria; and how students transition to their classes after the lunch period. Admittedly, that is a lot. But procedures that don't result in smooth transitions to and from the cafeteria can adversely affect the middle of your school day.

Q43 If bus duty is my responsibility, what procedures have I put in place to ensure structured and orderly transitions to and from the pick-up location?

In my first several years as an AP and principal, my district became a magnet school district. As a result, a small percentage of the students were from the school's surrounding neighborhood. A large percentage of the students were bused to the school from their respective neighborhoods (via buses in centralized locations on the opposite side of town). When the students arrived, I was there to greet them. On observing the students as they arrived, I noted that the high energy levels they displayed would prevent them from being productive during their morning classes. So I began my investigation into the cause of the excess energy levels with the boarding process. I discovered that the supervision at the pick-up locations was lax—there was very little structure and no procedures were in place—which the students took advantage of while waiting to board the bus. I immediately put simple procedures in place at the pick-up locations to ensure that the students conducted themselves in an orderly manner and, therefore, were mentally prepared for school when they arrived. I also spoke words of encouragement to the students as they boarded the buses.

If you are responsible for bus duty, what procedures do you have in place to ensure that the transitions to and from the pick-up location are as structured and orderly as possible? For those students who ride the bus, such procedures are vital to students' starting the day productively. It is imperative that this part of the day, which sets the tone for the rest of the day, be positive.

In addition to procedures to ensure structure and order, there is a need for procedures to ensure student safety. Are your students safe on the ride to and from school? Do they fully understand the significance of remaining seated for the duration of the trip to and from the drop-off location? Are the bus supervisors reliable? Do you continually talk to your students about proper conduct on the buses? Do you remind your students about your expectations regarding their behavior once they disembark? In large part, as the bus duty supervisor, the overall experience of the busing process rests on your shoulders. Be sure that you have sound procedures in place to ensure as smooth, structured, and orderly an experience as possible.

Q44 If discipline is my responsibility, what procedures have I put in place that lend themselves to a healthy school climate and culture?

As an AP, there's a very good chance that student discipline is one of your primary responsibilities. As I have stated throughout this book, despite having been designated as disciplinarian by your principal, if you are a supervisor of a percentage of the teaching staff in your building (which includes evaluating the progress of your teachers), it is non-negotiable and nondebatable that your primary focus in your capacity as AP is instructional leadership. However (again), if you are functioning as a full-time disciplinarian, it will be practically impossible for you to be the instructional leader that your students and staff need you to be.

As I've stated elsewhere in this book, a large number of student behavioral issues is a reflection of the overall climate and culture of a school. If student behavior is an issue, the school's climate and culture likely need to be addressed. As I stated in Chapter 1, I typically liken discipline to a micro issue and climate/culture to a macro issue. An AP and his leadership team can never become so consumed by the micro that they lose sight of the macro. The micro is the manifestation of a macro that requires your immediate attention. While behavioral issues persist, they, too, require immediate attention. To that end, what disciplinary procedures have you put in place? Are they known throughout the building? Are they consistently enforced and is there continuity across the building?

If disciplinary procedures are, in fact, your responsibility, you must ensure that well-thought-out procedures are known throughout the building by students and staff and that they are consistently enforced. When I think about disciplinary practices and procedures, I often think of the disproportionality that often exists in racially diverse schools: a national pattern (which some would term an epidemic) of students of color in general and Black and Latino students in particular being written up by their teachers, sent to an AP or dean for discipline, and punished by way of detention or suspension at much higher rates and far more frequently than their white and Asian counterparts. You must ensure that disproportionality relative to how behavioral infractions are handled is not present in your school's disciplinary procedures. You must ensure that all students are treated fairly and equally.

Consistency regarding how teachers handle behavioral infractions in their classrooms matters. If you oversee discipline and detect that certain teachers write up a disproportionate number of disciplinary referrals relative to their peers and that the referrals are compounded disproportionality along racial/ethnic lines, as an instructional leader, you must step in and spend a sufficient amount of time in the classrooms of the offending teachers and ascertain the reasons for the disproportionalities. Failure to do so translates to you rewarding the behaviors of the teachers.

Lastly, there are certain words used in education that I absolutely despise. One of those words is one that you may have noticed that I haven't used—*rules*. This word has been problematic for me for many years because it has a connotation in schools that is reminiscent of juvenile detention centers. I place "rules" in the category of deficit speech, which is reflective of deficit thinking—which puts students at a deficit. There is nothing motivating, stimulating, engaging, or inspirational about that word. My recommendation is to instead talk about *expectations*, *norms*, or *values*. I am recommending here that you create a schoolwide culture that embraces expectations, norms, or values. That is, instead of having conversations with students about not violating rules, engage them in discussions about meeting or rising to our expectations, adhering to our norms, or being mindful of our values. While this shift in language will be challenging for some, remember that we want to create a school climate and culture that are conducive to students being able to soar academically and personally. Toward that end, the language that we use matters.

Q45

What role do I play toward ensuring that emergency management procedures are developed and carried out with fidelity?

This is actually the most important question in the entire book. As important as student achievement is, *student and staff safety is the number one priority of the school leadership team.* Since the school shooting at the high school in Columbine, Colorado, in 1999, the world has changed. The education landscape has changed and, since that tragic day, school leaders had to ensure that they were fully prepared to confront or anticipate the dangers that could come to their schools.

While preparedness for emergencies falls in the hands of the principal first, the principal doesn't stand alone. The principal has a team and a staff. As an AP, you are a major part of the principal's team, which translates to you playing a significant role in all emergency preparedness procedures. As community stakeholders are involved in all discussions and meetings regarding preparedness for emergencies, you must participate in these discussions and attend the meetings. Your participation in the development of the emergency management procedures is vital. Your role in drills conducted to increase preparedness cannot be overemphasized. As an AP, you are an inherent part of the emergency preparedness process.

Districts, schools, and principals differ relative to how APs are or will be utilized regarding emergency preparedness.

As with all of your responsibilities in your capacity as leader, unless you are in a situation where your principal has so much confidence in you and your skill set that you have a large degree of latitude and autonomy toward carrying out your responsibilities, you are at the mercy of your principal. Not knowing your situation, I feel extremely confident and comfortable in saying that your principal is going to count on you and expect you to be an inherent part of the emergency preparedness process, which includes the development of the emergency management procedures. Because as an AP your "set of eyes" differs greatly from those of your principal, your input is absolutely vital. Moreover, I would dare say that you need to know your school's emergency management procedures as if you wrote them. Deep knowledge and understanding of the procedures is not limited to you; the entire staff needs to know and understand them. But, in your capacity as AP, your knowledge of the emergency management procedures is nonnegotiable. You won't have the time to reference the procedures in the event of an emergency in real time. As you, the entire leadership team, staff, and students must know exactly what to do in the event of any sort of crisis, you and the leadership team must drill your students and staff as often as is needed and possible.

CHAPTER

8

....

Planning, Organization, and Time Management Matter, Too

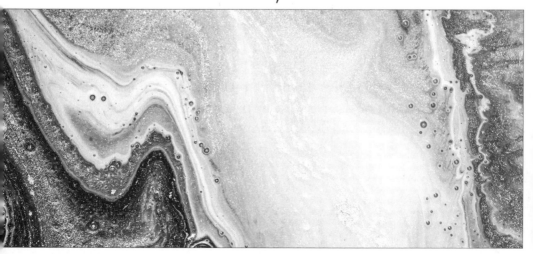

Q46 To what extent are my days thoroughly planned out?

In most districts across the United States, teachers are expected to create lesson plans. Although I have met a few teachers who disagree with the concept of lesson planning, I will continue to be unwavering in my belief in the power of lesson planning and planning for anything in life. (This book was thoroughly planned before I began to write it via an outline that I prepared over the course of about four months.)

In school leadership, daily and weekly planning are not always a priority. Many leaders walk into their schools and start leading without a plan for what they conceptualize that leadership might look like. I am suggesting here that, even in your capacity as AP, you plan out your week, particularly as it relates to the instructional aspect of your leadership. Instead of entering your building and letting the work come to you, plan your days and week out in writing relative to those things you deem must get done and when or what time they will commence and conclude. Most things in life should be planned for, as opposed to wished for or desired. Put forth a detailed and thorough plan for what you expect your week to look like and allow for the inevitable contingencies that will certainly arise.

Q47 Do my organizational skills allow me to manage and maximize my time?

Since enrolling in undergraduate school back in in 1984, I have prided myself on my organizational skills—which didn't exist before then. I had to develop them to get through college. They carried over into my teaching, my assistant principalship and principalship, and are critical in my current role as a consultant. Because I was highly organized, I performed all of the secretarial tasks (filing and retrieving documents), and my secretaries loved me for that!

Many marvel at how I manage my consulting business as a "one-person operation," which includes working with clients, booking all of my flights, lodging, and ground transportation, and writing up contracts and invoices—all while actively engaging in social media outlets Facebook and Twitter and continually blogging and recording You-Tube videos. I'm able to do everything effectively and efficiently because I am highly organized and, therefore, have the administrative aspects of my work down to a science. My organizational abilities enable me to make the most of my time.

How are your organizational skills? Do they allow you to get a lot done in the shortest amount of time? Do they allow you to manage and maximize your time? How are your time management skills? Have you mastered the art of maximizing your time so that there is time in the day for other activities? If you struggle with time management,

I implore you to thoroughly analyze how you currently utilize your time and make adjustments accordingly. Time management is an invaluable skill to have.

Q48 What roles do self-reflection and self-assessment play in my overall leadership?

Because I have written extensively on self-reflection and self-assessment in previous books, articles, and blog posts, I will keep the discussion of them here brief.

In the world of sports, review of the "game film" is significant in preparing for the next opponent after a game. Game film is the recording of a game that players watch after each game and for days leading up to the next game in an effort to study, analyze, dissect, and break down the plays made during a game. The intent is to ascertain what worked, why it worked and how it worked, what didn't work and why it didn't work, what needs to be enhanced, what needs to be eliminated, and what needs to be maintained. This study of the film serves as the basis of team practice in preparation for the next opponent. As a leader, you should follow the same practice. You must carve out time to deeply and intentionally reflect on your AP leadership. Going days on end without taking the time to "hit the pause button" and review your "film" is simply bad practice. You must thoroughly reflect on your day for the reasons that athletes study game films—to assess and evaluate your actions. Doing so will translate to you reflecting on and assessing your overall leadership toward ultimately making the necessary adjustments to improve your leadership. Like everything else I discussed in this book, the study of your "game film" via self-reflection and self-assessment are absolutely crucial to meaningful leadership and professional growth.

Q49 How well do I know my facility?

Here's another area that, although it may not come up in many graduate school courses, is significant. As a school leader and, in your case, an AP, you must know your facility inside and out. You must know your building as if you built it yourself so that you can act swiftly when emergencies arise. You must know your school's floor plan—where doors, closets, and storage rooms are, where the door to the roof is located, and so on. As well, you must have keys to *every* room in the building—the boiler room, the electrical room, the main computer room, the kitchen, and so on. Remember that, in addition to being one of the leaders in your school, you are one of the building managers in your school. Therefore, you must know your building thoroughly.

As an AP and as a principal, I knew each of the four schools that I led thoroughly. (After all these years, I still remember the floor plans and room numbers.) I implore you to know your buildings as thoroughly as I did. This is another nonnegotiable.

Q50 Does my "why" align with my principal's "why" for me?

In Chapter 1, I asked you, why do you lead? What is your *why*? As I close out *The Assistant Principal 50*, I want to bring this question full circle by asking you whether your "why" aligns with your principal's *why* for you. As significant as your *why* may be to your leadership, the reality is that you are not the principal of your school. You are the AP and you are there to assist your principal. Toward that end, depending on the leadership style of your principal, it may not be possible or practical for you to consistently walk in your *why*. However, I never want you to compromise your *why*. Walking in your principal's *why* for you is not a bad thing. Unless you do not aspire to be a principal, your assistant principalship is a stepping-stone to the principalship—a training ground toward preparing you to one day lead your own school. That may translate to you walking in your principal's *why* for you as you lean toward one day walking in your own *why* at some point in the future. Don't be discouraged. As long as you are learning, you are growing and preparing for your next level, when you will one day be the principal and perhaps have your own AP(s) to prepare toward one day fulfilling their dream(s) of one day becoming principal(s) of their own school(s).

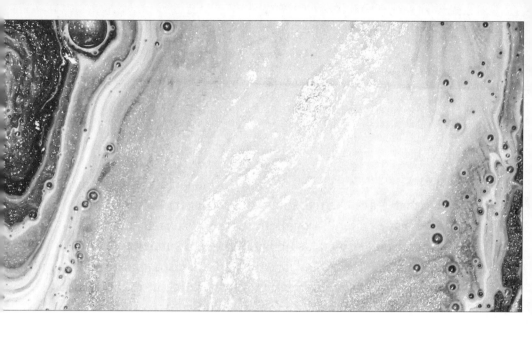

Conclusion

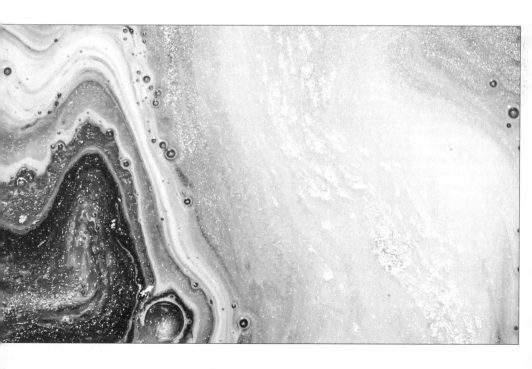

As I bring *The Assistant Principal 50* to a close, I can truly say that I am excited about the prospects for this book. As I have stated throughout, it is my strong belief that the assistant principalship is the most misunderstood and underutilized position in education. Assistant principals are, in far too many schools across the country, utilized very differently and too often underutilized. It is my hope that this book will play a significant role toward American education taking another look at how APs are currently being utilized.

Although *The Assistant Principal 50* is short and readable, I did not write it to be a quick read to be put on a shelf after you've read it. It's intended to be a guide and used as a reference throughout your assistant principalship. I therefore encourage you to keep it close by at all times.

Addendum:
Leading During a
Global Pandemic

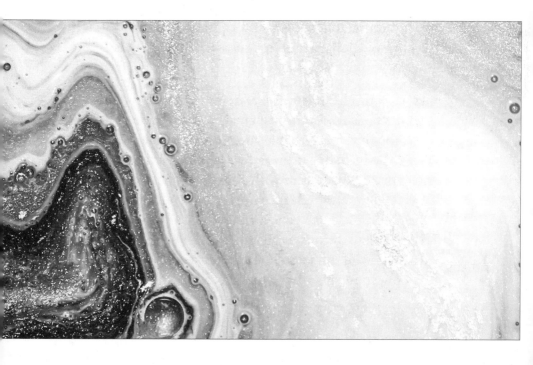

As I read the final edit of this book on April 5, 2020, we are in the midst of this unbelievable Coronavirus outbreak, which has forced me to think about educating children more so than usual (if that's possible). I've been particularly obsessed with how our educational systems will be able to sustain education for our children during this time in which we find ourselves.

As an assistant principal, it's unlikely that there exists a graduate school course or professional development workshop that could have thoroughly prepared you for leading during a global pandemic. You, like all leaders, have come to realize that leading students and staff in such an instance has to be learned "on the job" and in real time. While experts are providing guidance, at the proverbial end of the day, this is something very different. To that end, I offer the following as you continue to fight through this kind of global crisis in your capacity as an assistant principal:

➤ *Remember that your role is to assist.* First and foremost, your title is Assistant Principal. You are there to assist. Although it is admirable and commendable when you take the initiative in areas that you have identified, you must first consult with your principal. I cannot overstate the significance of you and your principal being on the same page during a global pandemic. Be sure to stay in constant contact with your principal (who is working from home). Your principal's home is now your school's main office. Keep your principal abreast of your thinking and the actions that you want to take *before* you take them because, remember, your principal is trying to figure things out too. This is new and different for *everyone*.

➤ *Support your staff.* As a supervisor of a portion of your school's staff, chances are that you know those staff members, including teachers, a little better than your principal does. You are the leader of the staff who report directly to you. They, too, are trying to figure out how to maximize distance learning while keeping their students engaged. You can never lose sight of the fact that teaching is a portion of their lives and that they have lives outside of school. In the midst of a global pandemic, teachers, too are dealing with the emotions that accompany the uncertainty associated with such an occurrence. As an AP, you must maintain contact with your staff beyond your supervisory role (it would be great if you could just check in on staff). Strengthen the relationships that you have with staff and let them know that you're there for them. Be sure to compliment, encourage, praise, and support your staff (via e-mail, department- or grade-level ZOOM meetings, and so on) as often as possible (noting that some staff may be taking the situation in stride while others may be struggling with it). To the best of your ability, be a support to staff.

➤ *Serve as a resource.* As an instructional leader and former classroom teacher, you are an academic resource. Although a plethora of distance learning resources can be obtained online, you know your students and staff. As, theoretically, you know what resources will best serve your students and staff, don't hesitate to offer your suggestions and resources.

➤ *Maintain communication with your students' parents.* Chances are that you communicate with more parents than anyone else in your school. The parents know you and you know the parents. Students' parents are as well dealing with anxieties and emotions during this kind of event. Many of them just want someone to talk to. Let them know that you're there for them and that they can continue to reach out to you via e-mail or ZOOM. As well, you can advise and assist your staff in engaging parents in meetings via ZOOM. Additionally, in your capacity as assistant principal, you work with a number of students, helped a number of students, and, likely, turned a number of students around. In light of the amount of time that your students may be away from school, much of what you established with them could potentially be lost. Therefore, I encourage you to communicate with the parents of the students you have worked with (and, if possible, communicate with the parent and student together [via ZOOM]) to ensure that your rapport with students is sustained.

➤ *Maintain a sense of balance.* I can only imagine how overwhelming the experience may be. You are in the position that you worked so hard to attain and then, suddenly, you are leading during a worldwide crisis. Despite the pressures and demands of your position, it is critical that you maintain a sense of balance. Your physical and emotional health is crucial. *Self-care must be a priority*. You must both work hard to make education work for your students and staff and balance your work life with your personal life. Your family needs a great deal of your attention. Attend to the needs of your family and *remember to attend to your needs*. Take time out for your own peace and never lose sight of the fact that you are not alone. Assistant principals all over the world are in the fight with you; you have access to them via social media (Twitter, Facebook, and so on). Communicate with as many APs as feasible, particularly the ones in your district and geographical area.

* * * * *

At the end of the day, remember: this, too, shall pass.

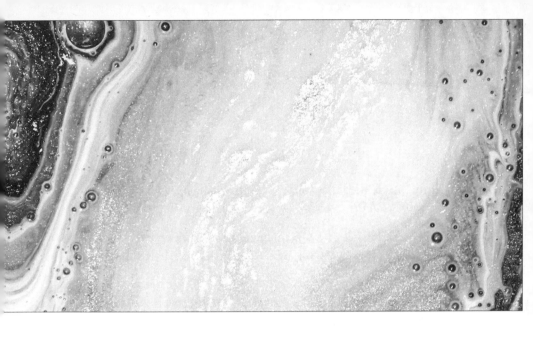

Bibliography

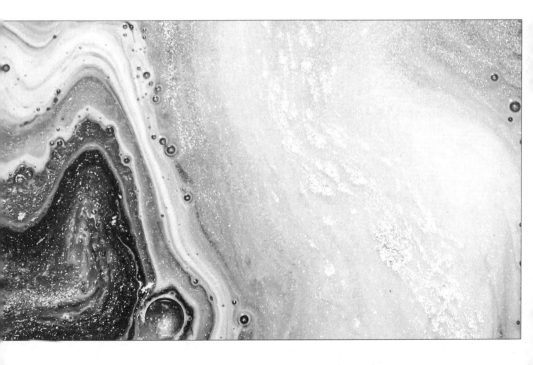

Kafele, B. K. (2013). *Closing the attitude gap: How to fire up your students to strive for success.* Alexandria, VA: ASCD.

Kafele, B. K. (2015). *The principal 50: Critical leadership questions for inspiring schoolwide excellence.* Alexandria, VA: ASCD.

Kafele, B. K. (2018). *Is my school a better school* because *I lead it?* Alexandria, VA: ASCD.

Kafele, B. K. (2019). *The aspiring principal 50: Critical questions for new and future school leaders.* Alexandria, VA: ASCD.

Lopez, N. (2016). *The bridge to brilliance: How one principal in a tough community is inspiring the world.* New York: Viking.

Robbins, P., & Alvy, H. (2004). *The new principal's fieldbook.* Alexandria, VA: ASCD.

Schwanke, J. (2016). *You're the principal! Now what?: Strategies and solutions for new school leaders.* Alexandria, VA: ASCD.

Sterrett, W. (2011). *Insights into action: Successful school leaders share what works.* Alexandria, VA: ASCD.

Thomas-EL, S., Jones, J., & Vari, T.J. (2019). *Passionate leadership: Creating a culture of success in every school.* Thousand Oaks, CA: Corwin Press.

Whitaker, T. (2003). *What great principals do differently.* Larchmont, NY: Eye on Education.

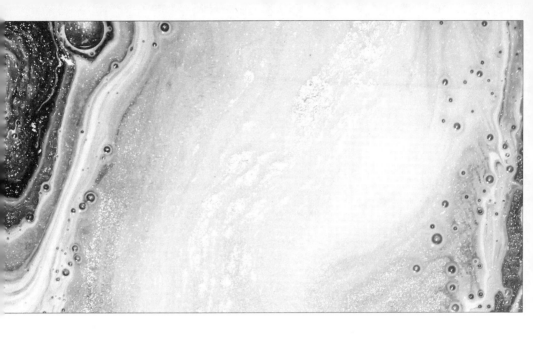

Index

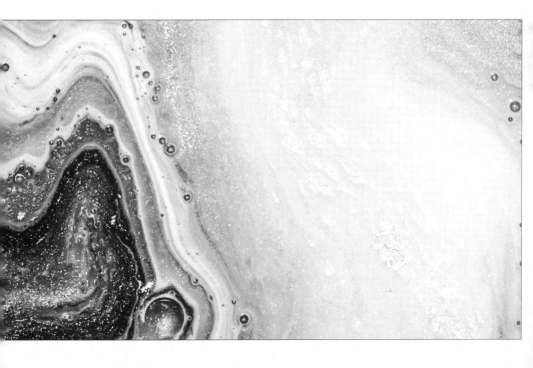

school district policies, 69–70
school-level planning, 76
self-reflection, 23, 90–91, 108–109
sign-in procedures, 95
social media platforms, 15, 32
Sojourner Truth Middle School Institute of Science, Technology, and African-Centered Studies, 90
special education law, 71
staff
    safety of, 102–103
    school climate and culture and, 45–53
    support staff union contracts, 72
staff meetings, 53–55
standardized assessments, 74
state content standards, 73–74
statutes and codes, 70–71
student learning and student achievement, 20, 73–74
students
    engagement with, 83–85
    safety of, 102–103
    supporting, 82–83

supervision of teachers, 26–28
supplies, 5
support staff union contracts, 72

teachers' union contracts, 71–72
teamwork, 38–42, 76
thought partnerships, 28
time management skills, 107–108
trust, 7, 36–38
Twitter, 15

unapproachability, 48–49
union contracts, 71–72

values, 101

why purpose for leading, 15–17, 110
work ethic, 12

Young Men's Empowerment Program/Young Women's Empowerment Program, 62
YouTube, 32

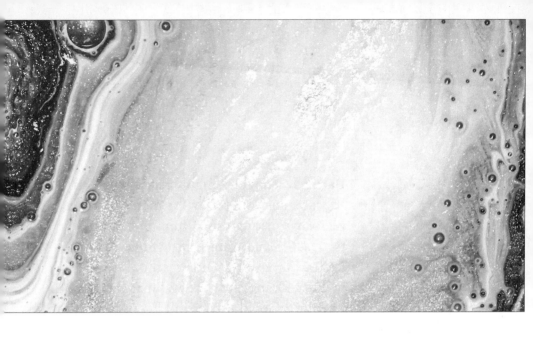

About the Author

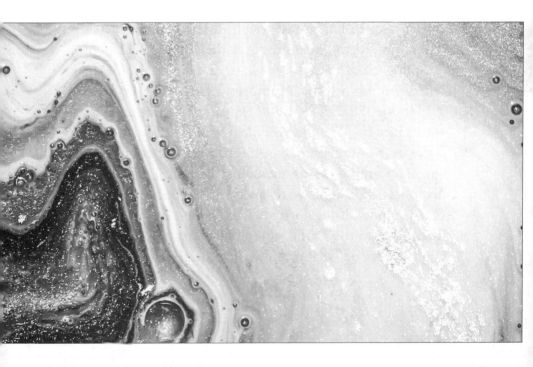

 **Baruti K. Kafele**, a highly regarded urban educator in New Jersey for more than 20 years, has distinguished himself as a master teacher and a transformational school leader. As an elementary school teacher in East Orange, NJ, he was named East Orange School District and Essex County Public Schools Teacher of the Year and was a finalist for New Jersey State Teacher of the Year. As a middle and high school principal, he led the transformation of four New Jersey urban schools, including Newark Tech, which went from a low-performing school in need of improvement to national recognition, and which was recognized by *U.S. News and World Report* as one of America's best high schools.

Kafele is one of the most sought-after school leadership experts in North America. He is the author of 11 books, including *The Aspiring Principal 50*, and his five ASCD best sellers—*Is My School a Better School BECAUSE I Lead It?*, *The Teacher 50*, *The Principal 50*, *Closing the Attitude Gap*, and *Motivating Black Males to Achieve in School & in Life*. He is the recipient of more than 150 educational, professional, and community awards, including the prestigious Milken National Educator Award and the National Alliance of Black School Educators Hall of Fame Award. He was inducted into the East Orange, New Jersey, Hall of Fame, and the City of Dickinson, Texas, proclaimed February 8,

1998 Baruti Kafele Day. Kafele can be reached via his website —www.principalkafele.com.